C000174025

Susan Sellers is the editor of the much-loved and bestselling *Delighting the Heart: A Notebook by Women Writers* (The Women's Press, 1989), and its companion volume, *Taking Reality by Surprise: Writing for Pleasure and Publication* (The Women's Press, 1991). She has published widely in the areas of literary and feminist theory, and women's writing, including *Language and Sexual Difference: Feminist Writing in France*, and *The Semi-Transparent Envelope: Women Writing – Feminism and Fiction*, with Nicole Ward Jouve, Michèle Roberts and Sue Roe. She is currently a Reader in English at St Andrew's University, and has previously taught at Cambridge University and the Ecole Normale Supérieure, Paris.

Also edited by Susan Sellers from The Women's Press:

Delighting the Heart: A Notebook by Women Writers (1989)
*Taking Reality by Surprise: Writing for Pleasure and
Publication* (1991)

Instead *of* Full Stops

a Guide *to* Writing *and* Publishing Non-Fiction

edited by Susan Sellers

First published by The Women's Press Ltd, 1996
A member of the Namara Group
34 Great Sutton Street, London EC1V 0DX

Collection copyright © Susan Sellers 1996

The copyright in each of the essays in this volume remains with the
original copyright holder.

The right of Susan Sellers and the contributors to be identified as the
authors of this work has been asserted by them in accordance with the
Copyright Designs and Patents Act 1988.

British Library Cataloguing-in-Publication Data
A catalogue record for this book is available from the British Library

ISBN 0 7043 4439 4

Typeset in Bembo by In-Type
Printed and bound in Great Britain by
BPC Paperbacks Ltd,
Aylesbury, Bucks

'Emily Dickinson'

Higgledy-piggledy
Emily Dickinson
Likes to do dashes
Instead of full stops.

Nowadays, faced with such
Idiosyncracy,
Critics and editors
Send for the cops.

Wendy Cope

Permissions

The editor would like to thank Faber and Faber Ltd for permission to reprint the poem 'Emily Dickinson' from *Making Cocoa for Kingsley Amis* by Wendy Cope, 1986.

Contents

Introduction   xi

- **The Subject**   1

  How to turn that idea into a book *Frances Arnold*   3

- **Research**   23

  Library therapy *Jane Aaron*   25
  Conducting interviews *Hanna Diamond*   35
  Preparation and flexibility: Keys to good fieldwork
  Heather Young Leslie   47
  Archive research *Wendy Mercer*   60

- **Organisation**   75

  Planning to write *Judith Baxter*   77
  Putting practice on paper *Gerrilyn Smith*   94

- **Writing**   107

  Writing non-fiction *Rebecca Abrams*   109
  Twelve 'rules' *Sue Roe*   126

- **Publishers and Agents**   133

  Contacting a publisher *Gill Davies*   135

It helps if you're famous: a literary agent's view
Dorothy Lumley   155
The legal side of publishing: Copyright and contracts
Lynette Owen   163

● **Editing**   183

Revising a first draft *Alex Bennion*   185
Layout and design *Christine Pedotti Bonnel*   197
The copy-editor *Virginia Masardo*   201

● **The Publication Process**   219

A view from inside *Moira Taylor*   221
Publicity *Karen McCarthy*   238
Sales *Mary Hemming*   245

● **Notes on contributors**   252

● **Select bibliography**   259

Introduction
Susan Sellers

Some years ago I visited a friend whose grandmother had accompanied her missionary husband to the banks of the Limpopo River in Southern Africa. She had left England as a young bride of seventeen, and apart from two brief visits home had spent her married life among the tribes-peoples of Northern Transvaal. The culture shock must have been immense. The eldest daughter of a devout widower, she had attended a genteel seminary from which men were banished and where gloves were required to be worn at all times. From this background, her new life among Bantu villagers must have appeared strange indeed. She took refuge in writing, penning long, lonely letters to her sister at home. The letters were honest, intelligent, detailed and witty. They told the complicated feelings of a colonial wife in a foreign land. As my friend talked about her grandmother, it occurred to me that her letters would make a fascinating book. I asked what had become of them. Yes, my friend sighed, her mother had considered sending them to a publisher, but not knowing how to go about this the plan had been dropped. The letters were left to moulder in a garage, until finally they were unreadable and were thrown away.

The story stayed in my mind. The letters provided a unique testimony to one white woman's experience of colonisation. It seemed criminal that they were lost for want of information about the publishing process.

Book publishing can appear a mysterious and impenetrable world to those on the outside. How many potential books never make it to the light of day because their authors give up in doubt? What is a good subject for a book? How does one go about research? Writing a book entails months, perhaps even years of investment: how can this best be organised from among the multifarious claims on women's time? How does one go about interesting a publisher? Is it safe to sign a contract? What happens to the typescript once it is delivered?

It is not only the beginning writer who may need help with such dilemmas. To the journalist, book publishing may appear equally unfathomable, while novelists may find non-fiction a rather different enterprise. Perhaps you are moving from one area of non-fiction to another. Compiling an illustrated history of lace-making is a far cry from autobiography or preparing a step-by-step guide to women's self-defence. Which is the best publisher to choose? Would hiring an agent help?

These – and many other – questions provide the inspiration for this book. Publishers and authors describe the publishing process – from the initial idea through to the finished product. Perhaps your great-great-grandmother left a trove of letters recounting in vivid detail her life as daughter of an Indian prince. Perhaps you are an expert in database programming and appalled at the dearth of accessible literature on the subject. Or possibly you have always been fascinated by town planning and feel it is time to put your research and knowledge to productive use. Does the fact that there is no decent biography of Fanny Mendelssohn fire you? If you have an idea you think might make a good non-fiction book, whatever your history or writing experience, then this book is for you.

Susan Sellers

THE SUBJECT

How to turn that idea into a book
Frances Arnold

> 'Everyone, they say, has a book in him [sic]. True, but
> in most cases it should stay there, principally because so
> few people have the ability to get it out of themselves in
> a form that anyone else will want to read.'
> Michael Legat, *An Author's Guide to Publishing*

There is, unfortunately, more than an element of truth in
Michael Legat's rather harsh words. Very few of us have an
idea for a book that will bear translation into book form
and, of these, fewer have the ability, knowledge and perseverance to get it out onto paper, into an eager publisher's
hands and onto the bookshelves. Even experienced
writers like journalists may find a sixty thousand word
book an enormous challenge. And novelists, making a
move to non-fiction, may find an entirely different kind
of writing much harder than they thought. But don't be
deterred. Plenty of people are able to 'get that book out of
themselves' – the shelves of bookshops are stocked high
with other people's 'ideas'. This book is designed to provide you with the ability and knowledge to do the same.
(The perserverance, however, is down to you!)

The main trick we have to learn when writing non-
fiction books is to change the way we look at our ideas.
We need to see them as potential, *actual* books, with a clear
and identifiable market and structured and conceived with

that market in mind, rather than as a mass of unstructured thoughts. We need to see our ideas with a publisher's eye, from a publisher's point of view, so that the idea can be shaped into something that publishers will welcome with open arms.

Publishing is a tough, commercial, hard-headed business. Most commissioning editors, those within publishing companies or 'houses' with responsibility for finding books and authors, are under constant pressure to 'sign up' or contract books that will increase turnover and profitability. They are constantly on the look-out for the 'big' book that will raise the profile of their 'list' and swell the company's coffers. You might think therefore that this would make it comparatively easy for an author, with an idea for a book, to engage the interest of a publisher. It is of course more difficult than this. Commissioning editors are in regular and frequent contact with past and current authors, as well as with potential future authors they are encouraging and, certainly in educational and academic publishing, are often to be found tirelessly touring schools and colleges, meeting new potential authors, following leads. They are also busy people on the rare occasions when they *are* in the office as they are responsible for overseeing the progress of books through the production process, liaising with their colleagues in the marketing, promotion, sales and other departments, dealing with authors whose books are 'in the press'. In addition, they must also constantly evaluate the audience, market and trends in their specific subject area by reading the specialist literature, talking to advisers and colleagues, keeping in touch with agents and generally keeping their noses to the ground. And they are *also* on the receiving end of a steady stream of unsolicited material, in the form of proposals, typescripts, letters and scraps of paper inviting responses to ideas. With such demands and responsibilities, most commissioning editors fine-tune their instinct and intuition when it comes to making decisions on unsolicited material, often reaching their decisions – for rejection, at any rate – after a quick read-through of a covering letter and outline proposal. Only a very small percentage of submitted unsolicited material (as little as 2 per cent, according to research) is accepted for publication.

The number of books published in Britain is incredibly high – over 88,000 in 1994 – and this figure is increasing every year. It is an enormously competitive market and you will have to do all you can to assist your project on its way. This will involve choosing your subject matter carefully, identifying and researching the market, establishing the correct style and approach for your readership, assessing the competition, and then approaching the most appropriate publishers with a clear, concise, accurate description of your idea translated into a saleable book project.

Choice of subject

Most non-fiction authors do not choose a subject, the subject chooses them. The idea presents itself quite clearly and naturally, and the author burns with anticipation about getting the idea down on paper. However, obvious though it may seem, it is worth saying that the subject on which you intend to write must interest you. A book written by an uninterested author is unlikely to be a good one, far less one that will engage the interest of a publisher and the eventual reader.

When choosing your subject – if it hasn't already chosen you – think carefully about your skills, strengths, expertise and knowledge. Are you an inspiring teacher, with reams of class or lecture notes littering your desk which could – with a little work – be put to good use as an innovative textbook? Are you often being called upon by colleagues and friends to give lectures/lessons/talks on subjects (managing stress, art history, motor vehicle maintenance) about which they and their audience know little and yet about which you are particularly knowledgeable? Is there a dearth of people who know much about this particular subject? Do you know more than most? And are there lots of people who want to learn about it? Have you travelled and brought back new perspectives on the world that we might learn from?

Then you should consider how much you really know about your subject. You will have to be able to convince the publisher that, not only is your idea for the book a good one, but also that you have the necessary credentials for writing it. In some areas of non-fiction publishing, most notably in academic and textbook publishing, ideas for books, in the form of written proposals, are usually sent out to reviewers who are experts in that field, for their comments and advice. Is your description of the biological effects of stress in your psychology textbook proposal likely to be accurate and correct? Do you know enough about all the artists in your chosen period of art history to pass muster with the experts?

Thirdly, when choosing your subject, think very carefully, and as realistically as possible, about its selling potential. Will your choice of subject be of interest to sufficient numbers of other people to make the idea attractive to a commercially-minded publisher? There are many ideas for books that should just remain 'ideas' (those books that are 'in everyone' and should stay that way); the life story of Great-Uncle Billy which, fascinating as it may be, is likely only to be of interest to Great-Aunt Jane and a few close friends of the family; or the enormously detailed history of the local village church which, while it may throw light on past lives of families living there, is unlikely to find much of a readership outside the parish. Ideas for books are all too often misconceived. Recently, I found myself chatting to a make-up consultant at the cosmetics counter of a large department store who, on discovering that I worked for a publisher, told me about her determination to write a book. I responded with my usual encouraging nod (you never know where you might come across a good book). On this occasion, imagining that she might be thinking about writing a beauty therapy book for trainee make-up artists – a very large and lucrative market and one in which my colleagues are particularly active – I encouraged her to tell me about her idea. 'Well, I thought I would write about all the funny things that have happened to me during my years behind the counter . . .' she said. My response this time was a rather non-committal 'Mmmm . . .'. Unless you are already a famous name, or have an outstanding talent for writing comedy, a set of personal anecdotes is unlikely to be on many people's reading lists. Her enthusiasm and interest in writing would, I feel, be put to far better – and more profitable – use if she were to think more carefully about her particular knowledge and skills and who could benefit from these.

Finally, is your idea 'big' enough to make a book? All too often, ideas don't translate well into book form. They are either too slight to sustain the length of a publishable book (more on length later) or they are overly ambitious. The former are clearly unpublishable and the latter, only slightly less so. The average magazine feature or an article, written for an academic journal on a specific area of research and about 4000 words long, is unlikely to bear expansion into a book of around 60,000 words – unless, of course, the article is based upon a much larger research project, from which exciting and far-reaching conclusions have been drawn. However, this is rarely the case. Just as a 'small' idea cannot be stretched to sustain the length of

a book without showing its skimpiness, a 'big' idea cram-
med into too short a space – a history of London in 80,000
words, for example – can run the risk of superficiality.
Alternatively, a 'big' – and ambitious – idea can all too
often become bigger in the writing, growing steadily more
complex and unwieldy, resulting in a vast, lengthy tome
that proves commercially unviable for the publisher.

So, you've come up with an idea for a book, on a
subject which interests you and about which you know a
considerable amount, and you're pretty certain a large
number of other people will be interested too. But are
publishers going to be interested in it?

What is a good book idea?

A good book idea is, to most publishers, one that has the
potential to make money. A book needs to cover its own
costs – paper, typesetting, printing, binding, payments to
freelance copyeditors, and cover illustrators and much,
much more – as well as contribute to other costs involved.
Nearly all publishers are looking for ideas – and authors –
that will sell in sufficient numbers to contribute to their
staff, office, production and distribution overheads, cover
royalty payments, compensate for discounts to booksellers
(usually somewhere between 30 and 50 per cent) and
wholesalers and distributors (up to 70 per cent) and still
leave them with a little profit at the end of the day.
Obviously the more commercial your idea, the more likely
you are to find a publisher who will be interested in it.
However, beware of assuming that an idea for a book,
because it is on the hot topic of the day, is necessarily a
good one. Unless the subject matter is so incredibly topical
and saleable that the publisher is prepared to lay out significant sums on producing the book very quickly in
anticipation that the costs will be recouped in large initial

sales, most publishers will look at a topical idea somewhat sceptically. Writing and production times are such that a topical idea is often distinctly *un*topical by the time it reaches the bookshops.

However, provided you take such matters as timing into account, tying your book idea into a specific event or celebration can be a good selling point, acting as a hook by which publishers can promote and sell your book; a book on women's careers, the launch of which could coincide with International Women's Day, or a text on the Children Act for social workers for publication immediately after the legislation comes into force, for example.

Perhaps more importantly, a good idea, from a publisher's point of view, is one that 'fits their list', one that will sit comfortably alongside the other books they publish. One of the most common reasons for an editor to reject a project is that it has nothing in common with anything else they publish. If they don't publish in that area, they don't have the expertise to market and sell into that area and nor do they generally have any interest in doing so. Rare is the publishing house that will take on an illustrated children's dictionary, however innovative and exciting it may be, if their reputation – and production and marketing techniques – was built upon publishing computing textbooks. Most publishing houses establish themselves, or are attempting to establish themselves, as pre-eminent in a certain field or fields and tend to concentrate their energies on publishing certain types of books that can be promoted and sold to similar readerships. A commissioning editor will usually reject out of hand a book idea that does not share common elements with other titles on her list.

Some large publishing companies, Macmillan for example, encompass both general – or 'trade' – publishing (fiction and non-fiction books for the general reader, both adults and children, literary, mass market and reference) and academic publishing (textbooks for students and professionals and high-level scholarly books). Other publishers concentrate on trade publishing only and others, on academic or educational. Within these divisions, books are divided into groups of certain types of books or 'lists'. For example, in trade publishing, there are 'lists' of fiction (including 'literary', crime, romantic and historical) and non-fiction (cookery, biographies, travel) and in educational or academic publishing, titles may be grouped into 'lists' of textbooks (sociology, politics, computing), academic monographs (history, literary criticism), English language teaching texts and so on. It makes sense to research your initial 'market' for your book idea – the publisher – very carefully. If you send your proposal for a first-year undergraduate sociology textbook to a social science commissioning editor within a publisher's higher education division, you obviously stand a good chance of your idea meeting welcoming arms! A phone call to the head office of the publishing company to establish the name of the commissioning editor to whom you should address your idea will take you one vital step closer towards publication. All too often, a letter addressed to 'sir/ madam' may, in a large publishing house, never reach its correct destination.

Finally, commissioning editors consider 'good' book projects to be those that reflect an identified need and fill a gap in the market; compete effectively with other books in that market; cover current and likely future interests; present interesting ideas in an innovative way; and appeal to a large readership or one that they feel confident of accessing.

Researching the 'market'

Any author-to-be should research 'the market' carefully, both the competition – what's already 'out there' in the marketplace – and the audience or readership. Most mainstream commercial publishers these days are becoming more and more 'market-driven', eager to match 'product' to 'buyer' in their attempt to publish the most commercially successful books; and other publishers need to adopt similar practices to ensure that their books reach readers and they cover their costs. Potential authors need to become similarly 'market-driven'.

First of all, let's look at the 'product' and see how important it is to situate your idea among its competitors.

(i) The competition

As we know, increasing numbers of books are published every year. Is your idea sufficiently unusual or different to fight its way among the ever-increasing mounds of books that flood out from publishers' warehouses into the bookshops? Why should a publisher consider your idea seriously? By the same token, why should a browser in a bookshop pick up and buy your book rather than another on the same subject? Is the story of your experiences as a trade union activist in apartheid South Africa any more illuminating and/or exciting than a rather similar book that was published last year? If you are planning to write a sociology textbook, how will your book differ from one of the leading texts, written by a professor at Cambridge?

It is worth spending time browsing at your local bookshop, public or university or college library, talking to booksellers, to friends who enjoy autobiographical books, to colleagues who teach sociology students, to students themselves, in order to refine your ideas about the readership, what the reader wants and likes, and the competition. As you pick up books in bookshops that are aimed at the audience for which you intend to write, look at their length, their style and content, how they are structured. Take time to study and read them carefully. Reading, in particular, is essential. As you read examples of other books in your area, you will see that most of them share common elements, and some may even follow a fairly predictable pattern; this will allow you either to adopt a similar approach or think of ways to differentiate and innovate. Would you approach the same subject matter differently – and why? – or do you feel it makes sense to follow the tried-and-tested – and successful – models of other books already published? Can you offer a new angle or approach in writing about your work in South Africa that would make it fresh and appealing? Perhaps your A-level Sociology textbook is going to have to cover all the core elements of the current syllabus, as does the leading text, but could this be done with more examples and exercises, more illustrative material?

Obviously, a careful look at the market may also affect your book idea. If you research introductory psychology courses, both by canvassing lecturers and students *and* looking carefully at the statutory requirements, you may decide to base your textbook on the most common and popular options, *as well as* on the compulsory elements of the course, and your research will have had a positive impact on your idea.

Having looked at the competing books, in terms of structure, length and content, it is essential that these are assessed for their strengths and weaknesses. Your book should, of course, stand up favourably in comparison to and, if at all possible, improve upon the competition. Could you make your structure more coherent, more immediately logical? Would your book be more appealing to students if the chapters were a little shorter than those of its competitors? Could you write more accessibly and more interestingly? Anything you can do to improve upon or differentiate from the other books in the 'marketplace' will help your idea become a reality.

(ii) The market (or 'who will buy your book?')

It is quite common for authors to overestimate the likely size of the audience for their book, which is perhaps very understandable and certainly not very surprising. However, most publishers are necessarily fairly knowledgeable about such matters as market-size and you should try to be as realistic as you possibly can, while still remaining enthusiastic about the idea! Just to take a few examples of over-inflated claims for market size: it is *not* true to say that a maths A-level textbook, even a superb one, will sell to each and every one of the students registered for the A-level exam every year (about 69,000 students); would that it were! Many teachers already have their favourite text, with their lessons structured round it, and are reluctant to change allegiance – or their lessons. Many students will share a copy of the recommended text between them or will pass copies down to next year's students. It is also unlikely, if the book is very closely allied to a particular syllabus, that it will sell to students registered with other examination boards with slightly different syllabi. An academic book on French cinema written by an English professor of French at an English university is very unlikely to sell to French students; they are much more likely to buy a French professor's book. In addition, such a book almost certainly will not sell to all students studying French at all levels, all those studying media or film studies *and* the 'general' reader interested in films, but probably only a relatively small proportion of one or two of these groups.

Most markets or audiences are actually considerably more specific than most authors realise.

So the author-to-be should try to be as realistic – and ruthless – about the likely readership as possible. As I've said, most publishers – if they are successful in their field – are necessarily very familiar with the market for which they publish and are unlikely to be impressed by exaggerated claims about market size. On the other hand, they *are* likely to be impressed by authors who show evidence of having researched the market, those who understand its requirements and needs and who are prepared to tailor their book to meet those needs.

For example, a book arising out of an optional – not compulsory – course taught to a class of third-year undergraduates with an unusual and idiosyncratic approach, is hardly going to be seen as a text with the potential to be adopted on large numbers of courses across the country. However, it is almost certainly still publishable, even though it may have only a smallish market as a supplementary book, read only by the author's peers and bought only by university libraries. If the author is prepared to acknowledge that the book is not going to be a text but is clear about the market, willing to write for that market at the right level and with the right approach, and if she then approaches the right publishers with the proposal, she is just as likely to get the book published as the author with that idea for a blockbuster maths textbook. Being realistic about your market and understanding your audience is vitally important.

Remember also that the market can be bigger than you had perhaps envisaged it. Many publishing companies, particularly in these days of large conglomerates, have overseas subsidiary or associate companies and/or distribution arrangements with other companies worldwide. Books are also frequently published as a joint publication between two quite separate publishing companies, with each taking specific areas of the world as their exclusive territories, usually with the originating publisher, or with the publisher who contracted the book, contracting for world rights and then sublicensing the US rights, for example, to a US publisher. Publishers are obviously anxious to sell as many copies of a book as possible and eager to exploit the vast international network available to them, to promote, sell and distribute books to the global market. If a book idea has international potential, most publishers are likely to view it more favourably than one geared solely to a possibly relatively small 'home' market. So, if while researching the market you have discovered that there could be enormous interest in your proposed book in the US or Australia (because there is currently no book available in these markets that examines whatever it is you are examining), make this very clear to the publisher and back it up with conclusive proof, if possible. The US particularly, with its enormous potential audience, can be a very lucrative market and if you feel your idea could translate genuinely into a book with appeal there, it is worth bearing this in mind while refining it. Incidentally, comparisons of the kind that follow, do *not* constitute an international approach: 'In the UK, and elsewhere . . .', 'The Clinton and Thatcher Administrations . . .' (the former would alienate US readers and the latter, UK readers). However, books that attempt to be, but are not, international, often fail both in the home and overseas markets as they fall between the proverbial 'two stools', so if your primary market is in Britain, don't be afraid to capitalise on this, A book that appeals to a specific yet wide UK readership – a British politics text or a text on the Children Act aimed at social workers, for example – can often sell in sufficiently large numbers in the UK alone to make it a very attractive proposition for a publisher. (It is worth noting here that even a relatively short, low-cost book – less than two hundred pages with no illustrations, cheap paper, and so on – probably needs to sell at least fifteen hundred copies to break even. If you think there is a demand for an idea because several people have expressed interest in it, be aware that the network this reaches may add up only to the hundreds, not the several thousands needed.)

You have now chosen your subject, established that you have the expertise to write about it and that there is a ready market – international or not – for the book when you've written it. How do you begin to develop it into book form?

How long should the book be? (or 'how long is a piece of string?')

When I was 12, in my eagerness to become a published 'author', I sent a story – or, as I thought of it, a book – to the then-director of Hamish Hamilton's Children's Books and received a very generous, yet honest, reply of which the following is an edited extract:

> Thank you very much for sending me 'Eagles Flight', I think it is a very exciting story but even so, I am afraid we cannot publish it. I know you will be disappointed, so I will try and explain why . . . To begin with, the book is far too short. Our novels are usually 160 pages long and never less than 128 pages and this means you would have to write between 50 and 60,000 words. You've only written 10,000 . . .

I won't bore you with the rest of his criticisms!

This was an early lesson, not just in the way one should write polite and encouraging rejection letters (he went on to tell me to 'read as much as possible, and analyse the way other authors write'), but also in the economics of book publishing.

So how long should your book be? This is rather like asking 'how long is a piece of string?'; it is very difficult to answer definitively because, of course, different subjects, markets and types of books require different treatment. There are no hard and fast rules. Most publishers, however, generally have an optimum length for a type of book, for a type of market, – as Hamish Hamilton's Children's Books did – so that they can produce it and sell it, at the right price for that market, at a profit. Any substantial increase in the length of the book increases the publisher's editorial and production costs. The most obvious response to this might seem to be to increase the retail price of the book to recoup costs, but if that price is out of the ordinary for the type of book, it is probably going to limit its selling potential. An unusually long book has to be unusually saleable, so that the publisher can print more and keep the price down, or, alternatively, has to be aimed at a specialist market which can bear the higher list price (a reference work for libraries, for example). Similarly, an unusually short book has to be unusually saleable so that the publisher can put a list price on it that might perhaps seem high in proportion to its length, in order to cover the basic marketing, warehousing and distribution costs and overheads (which unfortunately don't get smaller as the book does!).

So, just as books can be too long for their envisaged market, so also can they be too short. Very generally speaking, most non-fiction books are published at around 50,000 to 90,000 words. A practical text for busy – and underpaid – practitioners – for example, nurses or social workers – could be snappy, short and relatively cheap, while a work of literary criticism for an academic or library market could be considerably longer and more expensive. The length should ideally be a marriage between both the needs of the subject and the needs of the market.

Structuring your idea

It is unlikely that you will begin writing your book until you have tried your idea out on a few publishers and indeed it is not very sensible to write too much until you have established that your idea is likely to be of interest, that you are taking the right approach, that you intend covering the subject matter in a manner and form publishers are going to like or feel is required. Most non-fiction publishers are prepared to offer a contract to an author, even a first-time author, on the basis of a detailed synopsis or chapter-by-chapter outline and sample material, provided that they are convinced following a review of the sample material, of the author's ability to write well at the right level.

It is a very valuable exercise to start ordering your ideas, which initially may appear to be nothing more than a mass of seemingly unconnected images and thoughts, into some sort of coherent book form. You will be able to see more clearly how your book might fit together, where the gaps are and where you need to do more research. More importantly, perhaps, your idea will suddenly seem more concrete and real, more clearly 'a book'. So how do you begin to think of your idea in book terms?

Every book should have a beginning, a middle and an end; translate this into publishing-speak and the book should have an introductory chapter, a clear sequence of chapters in the middle and a conclusion. You have already decided how long your book should be; say, 80,000 words – or, with 400 words to a printed page, around 208 pages of 'book' – so you now need to decide how to divide your material up into manageable, digestible chunks. If you are aiming your book at a general or an introductory-level readership, you probably won't want your audience to be daunted by large sections of solid undivided text. There's nothing more off-putting to the reader or reluctant student than great lengths of dense type with no relieving or helpful section headings. In a student or general text, therefore, you might want to make your chapters as short as you can while still retaining a sense of structure and coherence so you could give yourself word limits for each chapter of, say, 6000 words and try to stick to this rigorously. Then, you will need to think carefully whether you will realistically be able to cover the particular topic in 6000 words; if you feel you're likely to have more to say, should you be saying it? Are you rambling? Is the material essential and, if it is, does it warrant another chapter? If you think you could only manage 2000 words on the topic, perhaps it doesn't warrant a chapter at all, but should be subsumed within another?

The structure itself – the sequence of chapters – should appear immediately sensible to the reader. Try to put yourself in your reader's shoes; how will the contents list appear to them? Logical, exciting, inviting? Will it include everything they are going to expect to find or are likely to need in a book of this kind? If you are writing a biography, which will almost certainly be structured chronologically, you could perhaps split the material into periods of years, or periods of the subject's life (schooldays, years living abroad, for example) or you might feel that the structure should be driven and governed only by what is interesting to the reader. You should at all times be thinking of your reader, your market and, of course, your subject.

Generally speaking, a scene-setting, ground-laying introduction is a good idea – establishing at the outset the thrust of your argument, describing the approach you are going to take, perhaps offering a brief guide to the reader to the material to follow. Following chapters could begin with good, sharp, anticipatory introductions, then divided into recognisable main sections and subsections through the judicious use of subheadings ('signposting' is very important); this will allow readers to identify particular passages of interest to them and will give further coherence and structure to the book. Each chapter might then conclude with rounding-up summaries or conclusions.

Considerations to bear in mind while structuring your book might be: is the organisation logical, useful to the reader? Is there going to be good continuity between and within each chapter? Would the inclusion of diagrams, or photographs, be desirable to elucidate or illustrate the material? Where could these most usefully appear? (But remember – illustrative material of any kind is very costly to produce. Some publishers rarely if ever use it. Beware of suggesting a heavily illustrated book to a small publisher whose other books don't often seem to use pictures. That alone could ensure your proposal's swift return!) If you are planning to write a textbook or workbook for professional nurses for example, you might want to include case studies, practical problems for solution; will there be enough of them? Should they go at the end of chapters or at the point in the text where the theory is explained? Should you include a list of further reading titles or a glossary of key words and concepts? Would your biography be made more reader-friendly if you included a family tree or chronology of life events? Or a *dramatis personae*? Should your self-help book have questions to consider or exercises laid out separately from the rest of the text? It is important to consider always your idea, not just in terms of what you want to tell your readers, but in terms of what they might want to hear/read and how they can most easily and enjoyably learn about it. Again, aside from ensuring a sensible structure and approach for the envisaged market, anything that can be seen as 'added value', that will set your idea apart from the competition, will – if it is appropriate – attract the attention of a keen-minded, alert publisher. Of course, a great deal of this structure may well change as you write, so do not regard your outline proposal as 'set in stone', but rather as a fluid and flexible basis for further work and elaboration. (See also Gill Davies' chapter.)

You have now established what you want to say, who you are saying it to and how you want to say it. Now – how do you sell this wonderful, exciting and well-researched idea to a publisher?

How to interest a publisher

As I have said, one of the most common reasons for a commissioning editor to reject a book idea – or a proposal – is that it lies outside their interests. There must be thousands of authors who have been on the receiving end of a rejection letter, saying: 'I'm afraid this does not suit our list'. It is important that you research your publishers as thoroughly as you do the audience for your book, so that you know which publishing houses are likely to be interested in your sort of project. At the risk of repeating myself, once again, a good book idea to a publisher is a well-written, exciting text that is likely to make money, or at the very least cover its costs, and one that fits their list. It is time-wasting – not to say depressing – to get rejection letters from publishers, particularly when this could easily be avoided with just a little research.

There are several useful and comprehensive guides, such as the *Writers' and Artists' Yearbook* and the *Writer's Handbook*, that list all the UK publishing houses and their areas of speciality, with details of the kinds of books they publish. It is a good idea to draw up a list of all those that publish books in your area – cookery or travel books, sociology texts or academic monographs – and then do further detailed research on these. Ring or write off for their catalogues so that you can get a clearer idea of the range of books they publish. Do they publish extensively in your subject area? Have they just published – or are they publishing soon – books in a similar area to your own? If so, they may be interested in building up their list with more titles along the same lines and may possibly look on your idea with favour. On the other hand, of course, they may feel they have too many titles on cookery or sociology already on their list to justify taking on another so soon. You obviously won't know their response in advance – it is difficult to tell a publisher's strategy just by looking at their book lists – but if you're approaching the right sort of publisher you can at least be confident that your proposal will receive sympathetic consideration (see also Gill Davies' chapter). Many publishers, if they feel your idea has potential, will suggest ways in which it can be adapted or modified to suit their list and will work with you to revise and refine your idea until it is in an acceptable form for publication.

Once you have done all this – thought carefully about your choice of subject, assessed the competition, researched your audience, established the length, style, content of your book, chosen the publishers most likely to like your idea – you'll be well on your way to securing that elusive goal; getting that book that is in everyone, that book that is your idea, your dream, out of yourself and onto the bookshelves.

RESEARCH

Library therapy
Jane Aaron

It is surprising what depths of self-discovery one can suddenly arrive at while immersed in the muted half-life of a library. In art therapy the client is encouraged to paint 'blind', as it were, and only afterwards appreciates the significance of the images unconsciously produced. In group therapy, members may be helplessly caught up in contention about the most trivial of issues, only to realise subsequently that what they were really at loggerheads about was a displaced equivalent or symbol of the unconscious tensions between them. Just so, to a researcher, tucked safely away from the outside world and its embroilments in some sleep-inducing reading room, can come unexpected revelations of the personal significance of their labours. In fact, it may well be doubted whether all the glittering prizes of an academic career (paltry as they generally are, of course, these days) would prove sufficient compensation for the months and years of immobile isolation which research in the humanities entails, were it not for such intimations. If we do remain content under such apparently life-denying conditions, we must surely be finding gratifications for needs which something hidden from us chose. At a subliminal if not conscious level, each and every dusty-looking reader, nibbling diligently away at their little protective wall of books, may be imbibing food for most intimate obsessions, quite other, perhaps, to the overt subject of the search.

In the absence of any very detailed record of the experience of others, I must put forward my own case history as an example of the practice of library therapy. I have so far had recourse to libraries over long periods of time for two apparently very different fields of research, the first being the lives and works of two English writers of the Romantic period, Charles and Mary Lamb, and the second, Welsh women writers of the nineteenth century. The first was not, or so it then seemed to me, chosen for any very good reason. Back in the autumn of 1973, I was still in a state of shock at finding myself living for the first time outside Wales. The new me – doing research! in Oxford! – didn't seem real anyway, so why not take up the first thesis topic which offered itself, which happened to be the Lambs: the supervisor to whom I was allotted was working on Charles at the time. Thirteen years later, with the thesis itself long past, I was still working away on 'gender and the writings of Charles and Mary Lamb' (such madness! thirteen years! – and three more still to come – on two minor essayists) when, one day, under the dome of the British Library, I suddenly realised why I was content to do so. I hope that it will not be taken as any disparagement of that worthy pair, nor raise doubts as to the objective validity of my own work on them, when I confess that it was for a personal reason.

My reading, on that particular day, was anthropological rather than literary. Charles and Mary Lamb were siblings, bound together throughout their unmarried lives by an unusually strong emotional tie. In order to grasp more fully the nature of their bond, I had ordered up a couple of articles on the formation of identity in cultures in which it was common for children to be cared for from infancy by their brothers and sisters. These articles stressed that the characteristic preoccupation of Western psychoanalysis with the infant-parent bond blinds us to the importance sibling relationships can have at formative stages, and described the differing patterns of ego construction and gender identity which result when a sibling rather than a parent is the first 'Other'. I was fascinated, but the images which kept coming to mind as I read were not those of the Lambs, but of myself and my twin brother, as we were back in that pre-school, oft-photographed, stage, when my mother liked to dress us identically. The connection was obvious enough, once recognised: at some shamelessly self-obsessed level, it was the particularities of my personal history I had been intent upon unravelling, throughout those years of supposedly disinterested research. My absorption in the Lambs' 'double singleness' constituted, in part, a displaced preoccupation with my own twinship. 'All literature is to me me', Gertrude Stein once confessed, but it's a bit of a shock to wake up after thirteen years and realise the precise truth of her aphorism.

But why should such an experience, enlightening as it may have been, necessarily be labelled *library* therapy, you may well ask. Was it not chance that I happened that day to be reading in a library? Could I equally likely have been visited with a similar recognition during the hours of more private, at home, study? Somehow I think not, or not at least in the same shocking – and thus more sharply illuminating – way. The sheer mass of hitherto unexplored texts at one's disposal in a library means that there one is more likely to come across the unexpected which will prove revealing. Our 'own' books, whether purchased or borrowed, have been chosen with conscious intentions which somehow seem to diminish their potential to be truly startling in this entirely unlooked for manner. What is more, we expect our hours in a library to be free of such personal intrusions: we expect a hiatus from self-referentiality, and therefore have no defences at the ready should it strike. And the self-imposed stillness of the other bodies around us, all no doubt containing equivalent mysteries of their own, seems to make the new discovery reverberate all the more eerily in our own suddenly expanded skulls.

Not convinced? Let me provide another example. It was also in a library, the National Library of Wales this time, that I first experienced a *felt* – as opposed to intellectual – sense of my reasons for working on Welsh women writers. This second research choice had, of course, seemed from the beginning a much more self-motivated and authentically personal one than the first: I'm Welsh, I'm a woman, I'm a researcher in nineteenth-century literature – ergo, I work on nineteenth-century Welsh women writers. But I had not started to plumb the depths of it before that memorable afternoon when I suddenly realised that the poem I chanced to be reading must have been written by my great-great-aunt. At the time, I was trying to pin down an occasional contributor to the Welsh-language periodicals of the day who generally signed herself 'M.D.' Up till that point, 'M.D.' had largely been interesting but as an extreme example of the difficulties of establishing identity when researching Welsh women writers. Born Margaret Evans, she had buried one husband, a Davies, then married a second, a Jones, and used all three surnames at the appropriate stages in her authorial career. The ubiquity of each of her surnames had reduced her to virtual anonymity. But now, with this poem, an elegy in memory of her brother-in-law, William Griffiths, chemist of Aberaeron – with all the details spelt out unequivocally in the title – 'M.D.' was suddenly revealed as family. My great-grandmother's sister – and I'd never known before we had a poet in the family.

My mother's relatives are not without pride in their

ancestors: a cousin went as far as writing a memoir of William Griffiths' father, a Methodist preacher. But no one seemed to know much about 'M.D.', although one aunt could verify – somewhat dismissively – that 'yes, Aunt Maggie did fancy herself as a poet'. In the struggle to give her changing name immortal life, Aunt Maggie, forgotten even by her own people, met with little success. Nor does her relegation to oblivion necessarily denote an aesthetic injustice, for it has to be admitted that hers is not a particularly notable oeuvre. Riddled as it is with morbidities, proprieties and sentimentalities, her poetry does not often rise above the common cliches of her period. Yet her unrememberedness and her anonymity, along with the obvious culturally-imposed constraints and timidities under which she laboured, make her career all the more representative of the lot of many a late nineteenth-century Welsh woman writer.

When I first began to research into these women's work, I was only acquainted with the names of – at most – a dozen or so authors. But as soon as I started to look for them, in catalogues, bibliographies, biographical dictionaries and the journals of the period, they shot out of the woodwork in abundance, wave after wave of them, all hitherto hidden from contemporary literary history. Within a remarkably short space of time, I had about six dozen names on my bibliographical lists. The history and achievement of most of these women is as entirely forgotten as that of my poor aunt. With only one famous exception (that of the hymn writer, Ann Griffiths), women's contribution to both Welsh and English language culture in Wales is commonly thought to have been virtually negligible until the twentieth century. Yet there they were, novelists, poets, essayists and dramatists, their works often sharply expressive, in overt as well as covert ways, of the gender and class repressions which circumscribed them. Theirs was the history of my grandmothers and my great-grandmothers, and thus my own history too. But I don't know if I would yet have felt the reality of all this quite as sharply as I now do if it had not been for the fact that 'M.D.' did, after all, dare to 'fancy herself' a poet.

It was in the library I found her, as I found all the others; she was submerged on its shelves, and yet saved by them too, her history overshadowed and at the same time preserved. A library is, of course, a very masculine institution, its stocks invariably heavily over-balanced in favour of male rather than female writers. Strict categorisation and rational order are of its essence — masculine attributes, according to gender ideology. The behaviour patterns it inculcates in its users are also redolent of the disciplined, stiff-upper-lip ethos. You don't readily break out into some such exclamation as 'Good heavens! it's my auntie!' in an academic library, however sharp the temptation. Yet, to a feminist researcher like myself, the tensions between the implications of that which can be disinterred in a library and the flavour of the place as a whole but sharpens the glee of a potentially subversive 'find' or discovery.

That is, if the said feminist has summoned up the courage to participate in the institution's rituals in the first place. When I mentioned the title of this piece to a friend of mine the other day, she assumed I must be writing about ways of overcoming a fear of libraries. She thought I was using the word 'therapy' as it is used in such titles as 'Behavioural Therapy', to imply a technique for breaking the grip of a phobia. In a way she was right, for an acceptance of my proposed argument on these pages — that all contented researchers are worrying away at something that is very personal to them — can revolutionise one's sense of the alien formidability of a large library. The reluctant researcher might, perhaps, imagine herself a diver sent to sea for pearls: somewhere in the entrails of that feared beast they lie awaiting discovery. Library can spell liberation rather than incarceration. But a library phobia constitutes a serious obstacle to such an enterprise, and one which can, of course, periodically afflict us all, whatever our experience or political orientation. Let me suggest, then, a step-by-step guide to ways of breaking through the library's alienating front and of overcoming any persistent phobic resistances. Behavioural therapies usually, I believe, work by means of such graded progressions.

Firstly, then, enter the library with a specific small-scale intent, which will help you to ignore the potentially overwhelming mass of it. If, say, you wish to research women writers of a particular period, and do not even know the names of these lost or never-found pearls, let alone their habitation, your first task is to locate the reference shelves. Biographical dictionaries are, perhaps, the easiest and most accessible places from which to begin such a quest. Explorers in this field have been much aided recently by the publication of a number of very useful volumes, such as *The Feminist Companion to Literature in English* (1990), compiled by Virginia Blain, Patricia Clements and Isobel Grundy, or Joanne Shattock's *The Oxford Guide to British Women Writers* (1993) and Janet Todd's *Dictionary of British and American Women Writers 1660–1800* (1987). A couple of hours spent browsing in these tomes is bound to leave you feeling that, had you but world enough and time, vast plains of fruitful oyster beds would be at your disposal.

Once you have a list of names, your next port of call could well be the British Library Catalogue, to check the data of your authors' book publications. Try not to allow yourself to be deterred if your library only has the computerised form of this catalogue rather than the printed version. These days, the amount of bibliographical material available on CD-ROM, or on the Internet online collection, is so vast, and so very useful, that it is worth the effort of becoming acquainted with these tools of the trade early on in your research programme. If your topic is literary, a search through the online MLA Bibliography for any recent critical articles on the subject is an obvious further step to take, for example. A new CD-ROM product, the Periodicals Contents Index, which promises 'comprehensive coverage of thousands of scholarly journals from 1800 to 1990', is also likely to prove a boon when it comes to trawling for any periodical articles published by or about your author. So watch out for any hands-on teaching sessions your library or academic institution may provide to introduce you to these resources. And make sure you get all the instructions you can – for exactly which key to press when – down in detail in writing. There's nothing so retrograde to the fruitful development of a library therapy of either the behavioural or the Freudian kind as wrestling with a machine which obstinately refuses to divulge its information. Invariably, on these occasions, the library's computer buffs are off duty, and there's not a soul in sight willing to admit that they might be able to help you.

But if no teaching sessions are available, or if the very thought of getting within hailing distance of a computer is enough to bring on an acute attack of library phobia, do not despair. Most research libraries offer the possibility of a member of staff doing the search for you and coming up with a print-out, though you are likely to have to wait your turn, and the service may not be free. And it's always worth going back to those reference shelves anyway, and hunting out further relevant bibliographies, like the *Cambridge Bibliography of English Literature*, for example, or, for contemporary critical material, the *Yearbook in English*

Studies. The printed word in handleable form can seem refreshingly pleasurable, in its straightforwardness and solidity, after grappling with the all too coded responses of a computer programme – with what unfailing docility the pages turn!

Once you have a title, of course, it's back to your own library catalogue, or to the Interlibrary Loan system. If yours is so rare a pearl that both these resources fail you, but you have the good fortune to be a member of that by now very scarce species, the funded research student, check whether or not you're eligible for a travel grant to take you to the relevant oyster bed. And then? – why then you open the shell, cut through the dross, and disgorge any bright seeds out into your notebook (computerised or not, as the case may be), taking care, of course, to check quotes carefully and be very precise as to publication details and page numbers, so as to avoid having to go through the whole process again later on. If you're not using a computer, it's probably still best, though expensive, to use a file card system to organise the pearls: it does make sorting out your haul later and reshuffling it a great deal easier. But what are seeds and what is dross? – ah, that only you and the hunches of your unconscious can decide.

At any rate, once you've got to that stage, you've probably seen the back of your library phobia. Further pitfalls of the irrational lie, however, in wait, and the most obstructive of these is the fear of closure. Drawing a line under each chapter or completed essay may seem a ghastly wrench. To such an extent do our aspirations unfailingly exceed our grasp that more can seem lost than gained on each such occasion. And as for submitting the companion of years into final bondage by a stranger's hands, be they those of the thesis binder or the book publisher, that can seem in anticipation like a death, as much to be feared as wished for. And the greater the unconscious contentment

34   *Research*

with the task and the personal involvement with it, the harder, of course, will be the letting go of it – as hard as quitting a good analysis. But take heart, there is life after library therapy. Or, if not, then there are always plenty of other fresh, juicy obsessions, waiting in the wings to whisk you back to those whispering shades.

Conducting interviews
Hanna Diamond

Interviewing can be an ideal way of uncovering information for all kinds of studies. This chapter will be concerned with showing how a series of interviews can be conducted. My advice will be based on research I undertook at the end of the 1980s on the history of women in Toulouse (France) and their experience of the Second World War in this city. My concern was to show what French women's lives were really like at that time and an oral study in this local context proved a valuable addition to other existing sources. Although a fascinating and valuable source, interviewing can be very time consuming. There are therefore a number of steps that I recommend should be followed in order not to create too much extra work. Firstly, it is important to define the task and your aims. What do you hope to discover? What are the key questions that you are aiming to address? It is helpful not to be too ambitious and to be quite clear about what you hope to achieve.

Preparing a questionnaire

Before starting the interview I recommend preparing a list of open questions.[1] This will help to structure the interview and act as a guide. In my case, the interviews were structured around a series of questions about women's experience of wartime conditions; their replacement of men both at home and in the work place, changes in their social and economic role in and around the family, the nature of the Liberation and the return of the men after the war.

My experience suggests that you need to be as flexible as possible about your questions. There is no point in writing a questionnaire and then sticking to it religiously, better to use it as a kind of check list of questions that you know you want to cover. It can be very frustrating to come away after a couple of hours and find that there is one vital question that you forgot to ask. I always establish the basics at the outset of the interview, recording the date and place of the interview, and then asking the interviewee some preliminary questions, their name, address, date of birth, profession, religious affiliation, marital status, number of children, education, etc. It may be helpful to keep these basic facts on record cards.

My interviews were very loosely structured to enable women to talk about what they felt to be important about their own experiences. Part of what interested me was to discover what had marked them in particular during the period and what they chose to tell me. Once their age in 1940, their family situation, their position in the household and their place of residence had been established, the interview normally took on its own momentum. However, the following questions were often asked to direct the interview:

• Did the Liberation bring any changes to their lives after the war in relation to their lives during the war? Where were they during the Liberation? How did they experience it?
• What financial resources did they have throughout the period? Did they work? What sort of work? Had they

worked before the war? Did they continue to work after the war? What did they earn?

- How did they deal with the problems of food supply, clothing etc throughout the period? Did they barter? Did the German Occupation of the region in November 1942 bring any changes? If they had children who cared for them? Were they at school?
- Were they involved in any groups or networks of other women? Did they have any contacts with what is known as collaboration or Resistance? How? What activities? Did they have any pre-war political experience?
- How did they experience the gaining of the vote? Were they ever a member of a political party? What were their experiences of the immediate post-war years?

Contacting subjects

This can be the most difficult aspect of carrying out an oral study. It is of course critical that the people you will be speaking to can provide you with at least some of the information that you are looking for. It is not always possible to establish this for certain in advance, but you do need to have some idea of the kind of people who interest you. It is advisable to approach organisations or societies, community leaders, libraries, etc for contacts. I also approached women at random through friendship net-works. It is always advisable to write or phone in the first instance explaining exactly who you are and why you would like an interview. It is best if you can give a name that they would recognise. I normally found that once I had made contact with one woman who interested me there was a kind of snowball effect. Each woman could recommend friends or acquaintances who would be interesting to talk to. I did also try using old people's or nursing homes, but this was not always satisfactory. On one occasion I explained my project to the director of the establishment and she was most enthusiastic. She set up a number of interviews for me, but I found that in interview the witnesses were often muddled in their accounts of the past. Women who had experienced both the First and Second World Wars, for example, were often unable to distinguish between them. So, in my case, I had to eliminate most of their narratives as unreliable.

How many people should you interview?

Depending on your subject of interest, you need to try and assess what represents an adequate sample for your purposes. It is impossible to establish exactly what a realistic sample may be as it depends on the context and the objectives of your study. I interviewed about 100 people in 14 months and used about 70 of the interviews. Some had to be discarded if I considered that accounts were unreliable or even fabricated. I did try to reach as many women as I could from a variety of different professions, social classes, and geographical locations (town/country) as possible. But, it has to be remembered that you are not really attempting to carry out a scientific study. The extent of the sample you use will largely depend on your common sense and the claims that you want to make for your study.

However, it is very important to describe the sample very clearly somewhere in the piece, most usually in the introduction or the appendix, and to introduce the interviews, giving as much material about them as possible, but also indicating where there are omissions. For example, I pointed out that the activities and war-time lives of women included in the sample should not be seen as statistically significant. The selection of informants was arbitrary and the fact that several were contacted through organisations meant that the sample contained a large proportion of women who were involved in Resistance activities or who were prisoner of war wives. Therefore the fact that 25 out of a total of 62 women were active in the Resistance to a greater or lesser extent could not be taken as representative of the population as a whole. In the same way, certain types of women were very little represented in the sample, if present at all. There were few foreign and immigrant women; there were no women whose husbands went to work in Germany and there were no women who admitted to involvement in collaboration. Such women were impossible to find. Furthermore, my sample centred around a specific generation of women who were between 14 and 40 in 1940. A few older women were contacted but their memories were found to be too unreliable to trust. The bulk of the information therefore came from relatively young women. Your reader needs to be aware of the limits of your sample in order to contextualise and interpret its findings.

Conducting the interviews

A little portable tape recorder is essential and it is crucial that you have checked out how to work it in advance and that you have charged batteries! Check it regularly. There is nothing worse than having to interrupt the interview to consult instruction manuals or fiddle with worn-down batteries.

Before starting the interview it is important to explain to your witnesses what you are interviewing them for and in what form the information they give will be published. If you are using a tape recorder, which many people find intimidating, you may need to explain that it is just a tool to facilitate note-taking and means that you will be able to concentrate better on what they are saying. It is a good idea to explain at the outset what say your interviewees have in the way their words are used. Reassuring them about such matters at the beginning can ensure ongoing trust and goodwill throughout the whole process. You should offer to send them transcripts of the interview and copies of anything you may write or publish as a result of meeting them. This is also a good moment to ask them whether you can use their name or whether they wish to remain anonymous.

The preliminary stages of the interview are the trickiest. I found that most women were unused to being approached and initially were quite sure that they had nothing of any interest to offer, perhaps because they were unused to being the centre of attention. Some even referred to their husbands as being better qualified to field questions. They found it quite hard to believe that I was actually interested in their lives and in what they had to say. However, in these cases, after a certain amount of time they gained confidence when they realised that their lives really were the area of interest. Most found that they had much to say and gave the information gladly. It is important to be as relaxed as possible and let the interview take its own course. Once the interviewees' basic personal details are established, it can be key to allow them to select the details they want to talk about. You can bring in your own questions at opportune moments.

It is usually best not to intervene too much and to feel free to return to points already discussed if they seem unclear or if you did not fully grasp their significance. And the more explaining people do, the better sense you get of how they think and feel. I was interviewing French women so I was often perceived as the English woman who could not understand the French way of doing things. My interviewees spelt things out in great detail and I received considerable additional insights into their view of events during the war.

My interviews lasted a minimum of one and a half hours and could last as long as five hours over a number of sessions. You may want to do follow-up interviews and these are sometimes more successful than the initial meetings because the interviewee has come to trust you and is at ease talking to you. They may also have given some of your questions more thought and have more ideas or information to offer you. Again, do not hesitate to cover some of the same ground.

It is sometimes awkward to know how to broach particularly sensitive issues or experiences without appearing to pry. I was often asking about the most traumatic and difficult times in women's lives. Many underwent extremely distressing experiences during the war. They lost loved ones and these were difficult memories to recall. Naturally, during the interview, women sometimes became very emotional and were unable to continue their narrative. Obviously, if an interviewee does not wish to discuss a sensitive area you must let it go, however important you consider it to be from your own point of view. In my experience, once the informant understands why these events may be of interest to you, and once they are more relaxed with you, they often feel able to return to the more painful, revealing or private memories, either later in the interview or at a subsequent meeting.

Imparting intimate and traumatic experiences to a virtual stranger is problematic for both the interviewer and the interviewee. I found that women tended to feel that by sharing their most intense experiences, experiences they found distressing to discuss, they had created a bond with me. However, it is usually impossible to sustain friendships with all the people you interview. The problem was compounded for me because many of my interviewees were quite lonely. I believe this to be one of the most difficult areas of oral history to resolve. The witnesses are essentially giving away a large part of their lives and not getting much in return for it.

Transcribing the interviews

Before using the interviews it is a good idea to write or type up full transcriptions of them or, at least, of the parts of the interviews that you think you might be able to use. (This is the most time-consuming and perhaps the dullest part of the process.) Obviously if there were subjects raised or red herrings that you know categorically do not interest you, it would not be necessary to write it up word for word — although omissions may need to be annotated in your transcript. One of the surprising things about interviewing is that you cannot always predict exactly what may prove useful. I have gone back to my transcriptions time and time again with different questions in mind and found fascinating material I had overlooked before. You may well find it very useful to annotate your transcript clearly and write full summaries, perhaps on a card index, of the subject areas covered. I kept a short life history of each witness on alphabetical index cards and then established a further reference system of key quotes arranged under the themes that interested me, for example food supply, the experience of separation, the experience of work.

   When transcribing their words, I attempted to keep the spontaneity of the witness' expression without making the material impossible for the reader to understand. Most witnesses were extremely concerned that I should 'tidy up' the way they expressed themselves if I was to quote them directly. This did mean that I occasionally changed tenses and moved clauses around.

In academic texts, intervention to make interviewees sound more accessible should usually be kept to a minimum. (In my articles, for example, I have tried to keep quotations in French.) In general trade books, however, more editing of interviewees' words may be necessary to make the piece read smoothly. This needs to be executed very sensitively, so that the interviewee's meaning is not changed or lost and a sense of the speaker as an individual still comes through the text. It is a common error, for example, to formalise interviewees' words in the editing process, so that important factors such as personality, race and class are lost and all interviewees sound exactly alike.

Feminist researchers have been very aware of how the transcription and editing process can distance texts from the interviewees' words and lead to their losing control of how their words are used.[2] The more you can do to reassure interviewees, and keep them in control of the process, the better, for both ethical and practical reasons. If interviewees complain, after the book is published, or at a late stage in the publication process, that they did not say what your book records them as saying, or that you have used their words out of context or in a misleading way, you may well be in trouble. It is important, if at all possible, to send interviewees their edited words, asking for their feedback and specifically for approval of any changes you have made.

Using the material

The way you use the material once you have collected it very much depends on the kind of study you wish to carry out. Life histories can be presented and then commented upon or material from interviews can be used as examples within the text throughout the book. I chose the latter, although I gave a brief life history of all the women I interviewed in the appendix. My study was not based on what the women had to say alone, but the interviews were an invaluable addition to the other material. In this extract for example, the witness gives us real insights into the way the Resistance functioned in the home:

> In my parents' house, my father was an official communist Resistance worker, so he used to have a lot of men and women visiting him. But it cannot be said that my mother was not involved in Resistance activities. Who used to get up in the morning to take care of the Resistance worker who was to leave before sun rise? Who used to darn socks and do the washing for the Resistance worker who was sleeping? Who used to prepare the food that he would take away with him? And who would be at home when the police called during an alert? I think that in my family, my mother was as involved in Resistance activities as my father.
> (Interview with Mme Dou)

The excerpts from the interviews really brought the historical accounts provided by the written sources held in the archives – police reports, administrative documents and the newspapers – to life. I normally quoted the women directly wherever what they had to say demonstrated a point that I wanted to make:

> Before the war, women were in the home. It was believed that a woman's place was to have children, to love and adore her husband and family, and to do the cleaning and cooking. A woman who worked was even quite badly thought of. But after everything I experienced of my life during the war, the fact that I had fought – I said to myself – I want to be someone in my own right. This impression I had that you can be a

mother but at the same time that you don't have any status annoyed me. And I think this was the case for many women who were involved in the Resistance, they wanted their value to be recognised after the war. (Interview with Mme Rivals)

However, there is some debate about the extent to which we can take what people say in interview at face value. It is evidently necessary to cross-check. In most cases we can check accounts by referring to other sources or by asking several witnesses to describe the same event. But how important is it for us to believe that we are getting a true account? Of course we cannot rule out the possibility that a witness may have a distorted picture of the past, consciously or unconsciously. We all know how our memories can play tricks on us. A witness may also have a hidden agenda of which we are not aware. But does it matter? The same can be true of written material. How is the memory of an event different from a subjective eye-witness account that we find in the Archives? Indeed are we looking for 'fact' and 'truth'? Does it matter even if this is only a representation of what really happened? Some feminists have suggested that 'the typical product of an interview is a text, not a reproduction of reality, and that models of textual analysis are therefore needed.'[3] It seems to me that the way you process your material depends on what you are looking for from it.

The experience of relatively small numbers of people cannot be representative of the whole. Interviewing gives us some insight into historical and contemporary events, but not the entire picture. For me, it is important to gain insights into women's lives as part of a larger project of gaining a better understanding of the importance of gender in our society. Women's experience is notoriously little recorded – the use of interviewing techniques gives us access to women's everyday lives in the past and present, it provides us with information we can get no other way. I believe that women's voices should be heard.

Material used in interviews can be used in numerous ways; it can bring history to life with incredible force and spontaneity. And, as far as the older generation is concerned, if we do not do it soon, it will be too late.

Notes

1 Open questions are questions that require more than just Yes/No answers.
2 See Gluck, Sherna Berger and Patai, Daphne, (eds), *Women's Words: The Feminist Practice of Oral History*, (Routledge, London, 1991), p. 5.
3 *Ibid*, p. 3.

Preparation and flexibility: Keys to good fieldwork[1]
Heather Young Leslie

For some reason, people seem to think that field research is a kind of extended holiday, or a romantic adventure, especially if it takes place overseas. 'What an exciting way to spend your life!' they say. I usually respond to their envy with 'Yeah, and working at McDonald's is a good way to meet people and learn to cook, too.' Field research is exciting, and fun, but it is also terrifying and frustrating. We don't call it field*work* for nothing.

There are many arguments for doing research in 'the field': journalists, biologists and environmentalists for example, and the most obvious, travel writers, have good reasons for conducting field research. For many people, field research evolves from some other project, spurred on by the idea that to better understand a people or a place, you have to go and learn from them. I do field research because I am an anthropologist and I am concerned with discovering answers to questions of gender, health and development planning. I have worked mostly in the Kingdom of Tonga. Tonga is a nation with a relatively good record of development in spite of a low gross national product, which makes it an interesting place to do research.

Fieldwork is commonly considered to be research conducted in a community which is not your own, for an *extended* period of time. While many people, like myself, do the bulk of their research outside their own country, the 'field' need not be overseas – it may simply be downtown. Anthropologists have been obsessed with fieldwork since Malinowski 'invented' it during World War One. Since then we have commonly anticipated, at minimum, one stint of field research, of at least a year in length, followed by several shorter return visits of a few months. Anthropologists have also been fairly preoccupied with writing about doing fieldwork, and some of my favourite readings on the subject are included in the bibliography. While I doubt that many people consider spending as much time researching as anthropologists do, the principles of getting to 'the field', conducting research there and writing about it are much the same regardless of time spent.

The keys to good research in the field, and good material to write from later, are preparation and flexibility. I'll briefly cover the areas to consider when planning field research, move on to writing research proposals and field notes, and give some examples from my own time in the field.

Unless you are being sent by an employer, or are independently wealthy, you'll probably need funding for your research. However, funding, the thing we all think of first, is the last step in a series of preparations for conducting fieldwork. Before you can even apply for research funds, you need a research proposal. Before you can write a proposal, you must be prepared intellectually: so field research must be preceeded by library and archive work.

While you are preparing yourself intellectually, you must also prepare yourself physically and mentally. If you are planning overseas fieldwork I recommend you make your medical visits at least four months before you plan to depart: some innoculations must be spaced over several weeks, and you want to fit them all in. Travel insurance is a must, but so is good general physical condition: you might need to walk the equivalent of several city blocks carrying a heavy pack, or sit and sleep on a bare floor; you may have trouble staying on a special diet, if you plan to be in areas that don't usually cater to your needs.

A vital part of your planning is the mental preparation. One of the most important lessons drilled into every aspiring field researcher's head is about the problems caused by ethnocentrism. Ethnocentrism refers to the belief that one's own way of doing something is the best system. This is ethically unacceptable, factually incorrect and the surest way to ruin your field research, whether it is in Tonga or Twickenham! While it is important to hold to your own sense of who you are, and what you think is right, it is also vital to remember that your ideas are particular to you and your own social milieu. They may not hold true, in fact may be dangerous or ridiculous in another social setting. The old adages about 'when in Rome', and 'do not judge lest you be judged' are valuable prescriptions for avoiding problems related to ethnocentrism. If you can manage it, a course dealing with issues of cultural sensitivity and adapting to a foreign environment would be invaluable.

When you enter a new and different environment or social setting, regardless of whether you are conducting research overseas or in a different part of the country, you also need to be prepared to experience some stress due to the unfamiliar circumstances. When this stress is severe, as it can be if you plan on being in the field for an extended period of time, we call it culture shock. Culture shock is no laughing matter; it's much more serious than simple homesickness. I've known it to ruin relationships and cause illness. Being in culture shock can make you feel depressed, angry, irritable, afraid, sad, suspicious, frustrated, and tired; a lack of appetite and insomnia or nightmares are also fairly common. Understanding that this is a normal circumstance helps. So does knowing as much as possible about the place you are going to be doing your research in, and doing your best to learn local habits.

All of this preparation takes time, time that is very important. Don't cheat yourself by skimping on your preparation time. Just for comparison, consider that most anthropologists take three to five years preparing for their first fieldwork experience whether they are doing local or overseas research. On the other hand, it's common to concentrate more than necessary on material things when you're thinking of travelling far. First-aid kits, changes of clothing and adequate reading material tended to pre-occupy me on my first field trip. I took unnecessary drugs, which I ended up giving away, books which I never got the chance to read, and I ended up buying more appropriate local clothing. My best advice here is that less is more. I doubt that there is any capital city of any country with an airport, that doesn't have shops where you can purchase the items you'll need for day-to-day living. A recent edition of a travel guide, like the ones published by Lonely Planet, is useful for tips about travel to unfamiliar locales. It's also a good idea to talk to someone who has done research in the same place if you can. Consulate or embassy representatives will be able to offer advice. You may have to talk to them to get a travel visa or research permit anyway (I'll discuss permits below). But be aware that diplomatic officials will tend to overdramatise the discomforts and underestimate your ingenuity.

Eventually after your library, archive and medical preparations, and learning what you can about the social practices of your destination, you come to the point of asking for funding. This leads me to the writing of research proposals.

There are roughly two types of research proposals:

applications for financial support, and permission to conduct research. The former usually go to agencies, but can really be sent to anyone you think will give you money (Nick Danziger's book, *Danziger's Travels*, discusses the varieties of people he approached for sponsorship to travel from London to Beijing by land: it's a fun read!). The permission proposals go to government offices: via a consulate, an embassy, or directly to a ministry office in the country where you wish to conduct research.

Research proposals to funding agencies have a surreal quality to them. They are condensed nuggets of future-oriented prose, where speculation is disguised as certainty, and self-promotion must be subtle but definite. It's a strange process. The sub-text of a funding proposal is always the same: 'This bit of research is important to the future of scholarship, perhaps even the world. It must be done, and I am the *best* person to do it.'

I never *really* believe that (although I want to!), even when I'm busy trying to convince the unknown evaluators of it. Usually, what I want to say is 'Look, I'm smart, I work hard; you've funded all sorts of stupid research and given money to people who say they'll do one thing and then go ahead and do another; you've funded other people not as sincere or ethical about their research as me, so acknowledge my integrity and hard work and just *give me the money* so I can carry on!' But that kind of bald reality is unacceptable – too far outside the rules. So when I write research proposals, I pretend I'm in a ritual drama; I'm a supplicant using eloquence, key phrases and just a hint of emotional manipulation to convince the committees to sponsor my work.

Whether or not it's true I don't know (except that I have been fairly successful at getting funding), but it seems to me that the thing to do is to find out what the funding bodies want to hear, and then tell them that is what you are going to do. The process is similar to the way I write stories for my daughter: 'give me four things to put in the story' I tell her, and she gives me a list: 'a bunny, a princess, a castle, a turtle'. With research proposals, the process is the same, only the ingredients differ: 'women, health, rural, community', or 'practice, resistance, discourse, indigenous'. It's unfortunate but true that the key words go in and out of fashion, as agencies, governments and donors change their funding priorities. Your challenge is to frame your very important research questions in terms that meet their very important research priorities.

Usually, a funding proposal has several different drafts and versions, depending upon the intended audience. The Social Sciences and Humanities Research Council in Canada, for instance, offers awards based on a page and a half description of the project; they offer a fixed sum of money and don't want to see a budget. But the International Development and Research Centre and CIDA (both development agencies based in Canada) require a proposal of about ten pages and a detailed budget.

Furthermore, funding bodies tend to be nationalistic and topic specific. Arts councils fund certain kinds of research, not funded by social science councils or development centres and most funding bodies will only fund citizens of their country. Your public library will have a section which lists funding bodies, and their guidelines. That information is invaluable if you need to apply for research funds.

It's important to remember that there is a seasonality to proposal viewing. This means that whoever is reading your proposal is reading many others at the same time. Reviewers get tired, and that makes them cranky. They look for detail and directness, and appreciate clear prose, without jargon. Generally, the shorter your proposal, the better.

Proposals for permission to conduct research are addressed to a different audience. Government ministries wanting to screen researchers may want a longer, more detailed proposal, say ten to twenty pages. The proposal I sent to the Kingdom of Tonga for research I conducted there in 1991 was twenty pages long. It included a five-page review of previous research, and a detailed description of what methods and questions I would be using, as well as how much money I would be spending ($30,000 Canadian), how many people I might hire as assistants or translators (four to six), and the value to the world community of the project: 'Tonga provides a fine example of development with limited resources.'

These ministries also operate on a very different schedule. Funding proposals usually get a response in something like six months, maybe less. I began negotiating the convoluted process of receiving a cabinet order granting permission to do research in His Majesty's Kingdom of Tonga in 1989. After my letters and faxes, I began to phone, getting up at three o'clock in the morning to get the office staff in Tonga before their coffee break. I received permission just before leaving Canada in late summer 1991.

Regardless of who the proposal is for, it is important to write well, displaying good grammar and a broad vocabulary. It's also necessary that you demonstrate a comprehensive understanding of the topic. This means citing the proper scholarly references. Yet you need to be innovative. It may help to include some poetry or literature, or draw a connection between two previously unconnected discourses.

Obviously I used different versions of the same proposal, for each of the different readers. So while I wrote one basic proposal, each one required its own special fine tuning, according to its specific audience. Fine tuning is an essential skill, but easy to learn: after I'm satisfied with the content and length of a proposal, I go over the text with several fine-toothed, merciless combs. I remove *every* unnecessary word. For instance I could have said 'I remove every single unnecessary word.' But 'single' is not essential to the meaning of the sentence. So out with it! The next step is to change all indefinite phrases to definite ones: 'I will', not 'I hope to'. Keep the sentences short, but not cryptic. Then check the spelling, the grammar and even the printer font, to make sure there are no little flaws to irritate the evaluating committee. When I can do nothing more, I get a second opinion on the readability and clarity. If I'm not pressed by a looming deadline, I'll shelve the proposal for three days, to let my brain relax. When I go over it with fresh eyes, I read it aloud to myself, looking again for flaws. If I'm satisfied after this second reading, away it goes, with fingers crossed for good luck.

The thing to remember about funding proposals is this: your application is being judged against a pool of applicants. If your research project is not funded, it doesn't mean that the idea is foolish, or that your proposal was bad, or that you are in some way inferior. It just means that the evaluators liked someone else's proposal better, *in that round*. So don't give up! If you don't get funding or permission, try somewhere else. When it comes to funding, I'm reminded of the inspiration of two women: Dr Ruth Landes, and Dr Emöke Szathmáry. Early in her career, Dr Landes' applications to funding agencies for a research project she planned for Brazil were refused. Rather than give up, she just tried another angle: she listed the multinational corporations working in Canada and Brazil, and made appointments with some Vice Presidents. She convinced them of the importance of her research, reminded them of their civic duty to the nation providing their company with labourers and resources and got her funding. Her book, *City of Women*, was a groundbreaking analysis of prostitutes' lives. Dr Szathmáry was my first professor as an undergraduate and I idolised her. I suffered terribly, trying to master population genetics just so that I could take her classes. She always made her students apply for every possible source of funding: 'The more you try, the better your chances of winning,' she'd say. I never did master genetics, but I've done well with her other lesson.

In 1991, I went to Tonga to do research into maternal health practices. The research period of a year or more, living as a member of the community is, as I've mentioned, a standard anthropological method. Like many anthropologists, the selection of my 'field site' was serendipitous, and my experience indicates the need for flexibility when doing fieldwork.

I had planned to do research on maternal and child health issues among highland people in Papua New Guinea. But in 1988, civil war erupted in Papua New Guinea, sparked by turmoil over land tenure and international mining on the island of Bouganville. Reports of vandalism rose dramatically. Europeans and their local associates were reported as targets, due to the assumption that they were likely to have cash. My department responded to this panic with the statement 'no research is worth the life of the researcher or their associates'. Suddenly Papua New Guinea was out. These kinds of last-minute hitches should not be viewed negatively, as they may open up unanticipated options: as unexpectedly as the civil strife scare erupted I learned that the king of Tonga wished to encourage research. I was obliged to repeat the literature search, and rewrite my proposals to reflect the particular needs of the Tongan peoples, but my overall questions of maternal health remained unchanged. Flexibility? It's my middle name!

Tongans are a Polynesian people, descendents of

seafaring explorers who criss-crossed the Pacific in huge, double hulled canoes, establishing complex societies on numerous volcanic islands and coral atolls centuries some 3200 years ago. Today, Tongans living in the kingdom number approximately 100,000, but most families have relatives living in large cosmopolitan cities, such as Auckland, Los Angeles, or Honolulu. The kingdom consists of 173 islands and the surrounding ocean. The economy is mostly subsistence-oriented: most men farm, fish and raise livestock for food. They give, trade or sell any surplus. Women make barkcloth or fine-plaited mats, go reef-fishing, and nurture the many children and churches.

Because it is an island nation, problems relating to regional disparity are numerous. This was the basis for my research questions: on islands where it is difficult to access medical treatment, where there is no wage employment, secondary school, refrigeration, or ground water, what do women do about their children's health care? How effective has the World Health Organisation been in rural Tonga? What are the ramifications of women's daily practices for their children's health? What do people understand 'health' to be – how do they identify it? How is it that isolation and poverty aren't associated with high levels of maternal or infant morbidity, as they are in other countries? What I found was that, for the rural Tongan people I lived among, 'health' was defined primarily as evidence of good familial and social relationships. With regard to women's and children's health, secure land tenure, familial control over crop production, high status of women as sisters, desire for children of either sex, a safe environment and benign government are probably more important then the interventions of medical personnel and health development projects.

So what does one do when 'in the field'? In many circumstances, the first task is to learn the language and appropriate social behaviours: you can't do good fieldwork if you can't talk to people and understand them when they try to talk to you. During this phase, I was also introducing myself to the community and explaining the research project. Eventually, I began to make contacts, conduct interviews and record coherent observations. That's where field notes become important. It is essential to write things down while they are fresh: good notes in the field allow you continually to reconsider your research design, the questions you're asking and the approach you're taking. Without them, it's hard to achieve the self-critical position necessary to decide if you need to change your research focus in order to reflect the realities of your research subjects. Because you must be prepared to let the people you are interviewing have their say in the research, too. (There is a great deal of literature dealing with the problem of recording data and revising the research focus, and one particularly useful book is Robert Burgess' *In the Field: An Introduction to Field Research* (see bibliography)).

Here I'd like to point out an overlooked tool in fieldwork: the sketch pad. Sketching allows you to be both listener and recorder, in a way that is much more intimate, and less alienating than written notes or camera. It allows the 'subjects' immediate entry into the researcher's work. Because they can see what you're doing, it's much more accessible than writing in a different language or taking a photograph, which takes weeks or months to be developed. Sketching also makes you slow down, and *really* pay attention. This often has the added benefit of making you listen as well as look, and doesn't preclude your stopping to talk. This is especially useful when you are still at the language acquisition stage. You can pause to show your work to a curious person, and let your drawing spark conversation on the subject matter of the sketch. Even if you are not an 'artist', the process of trying to sketch offers the rewards of making you pay attention in ways you may not otherwise do.

One of the hardest tasks during fieldwork is balancing your time: there is so much to write down, so much to ask, so much to learn. But you also need time to relax and enjoy yourself. Denying yourself pleasure and fun during this very intense experience can be dangerous to your health, not to mention your sanity. Besides, being a fieldworker is a job that is inherently humorous, if you take the right perspective: there are few other kinds of work where you can anticipate being ridiculous, on a daily basis!

Imagine, if you will, a stranger knocking on *your* door, and asking if they could spend the day with you, measuring your food or work materials, watching you as you work (or relax), observing your family interactions and asking interminably silly questions. That's what I do. Sometimes, people refused. Often, they laughed at my clumsiness or confusion. Most of the time though, I was the recipient of a great deal of co-operation, affection and attention. Seeing oneself as equally comic relief and the recipient of great generosity is a humbling experience.

Doing field research is a privilege, but it is not a vacation. As a learning experience I rank it up there with childbirth: it's painful, frightening, exciting and rewarding. You can describe it until you are blue in the face, but nothing offers so much scope for thinking and writing as experiencing it for yourself.

Notes

1 The research upon which this article is based was funded by the International Development and Research Centre, Ottawa, Canada, as a Young Canadian Research Fellowship awarded in 1991. I am indebted to the Cabinet of His Majesty, King Taufa'ahau Tupou IV for permission to

conduct research in the Kingdom of Tonga from 1991 to 1993. 'Oku lahi'ange he'eku fatongia kia he toko lahi 'oe kolo 'oe Maka Fele'unga. Fakatapu kiate moutolu, 'e 'ofa lahi atu.

Archive research
Wendy Mercer

Archive work may, to the uninitiated, sound daunting, inaccessible, frustrating or just plain boring. To be perfectly honest, it is often all of these for long stretches of time: and yet there is nothing, for me, to match the satisfaction, indeed the thrill, of uncovering that elusive date, the lost letter, the unsuspected document or mere comment which can lead to far wider and unexpected fields of discovery. Following up clues in archives and unravelling a story – or indeed, discovering a whole new story whose existence you never even suspected – is like starring in your very own real-life detective novel. My own experience with archive work has shown that when you go in search of one piece of data, you will more often than not find whole reams of unexpected material opening up before you.

The term 'archive' is very broad. I shall use it here in general terms, to designate any collection of records or manuscript material. Under this heading one might include anything from the manuscript of a well-known literary text to a birth certificate, from a police or prison record to an employment file, or even a collection of private letters. Whatever the subject you have chosen, be it a biography, an edition of a literary text – or even a new edition of a manual on the internal combustion of the jet engine – a thorough job very often involves manuscript (unpublished) material at some stage in the process, for reasons which will become clear. You will probably only seek out unpublished material after you have exhausted all the published sources. Yet even if you *expect* to find nothing new (from the manuscript of a text that has already been published for example), you may well be surprised.

I learned this lesson early on in the course of my documentation for the biography of Xavier Marmier, a Frenchman who lived through most of the nineteenth century. He was a traveller, a linguist and an influential writer who became famous and was nominated to the French Academy for exploring and studying previously undocumented countries, and writing about them in books and newspaper articles. Despite the fame he achieved during his lifetime, his name was largely forgotten until a Canadian researcher published Marmier's personal papers in 1968. The publication of this journal generated an enormous interest in the press and in the academic world, as it shed new light on many events of the 1848 revolution in Paris, which deposed the king, Louis-Philippe, and sparked off a series of revolutions across Europe, the siege of Paris in the Franco–Prussian war (and the conditions of privation endured by even the wealthiest), the Commune (the short-lived revolutionary government of France so brutally suppressed by the troops of Thiers in 1871), and so on. Because Marmier was a prominent character, he knew many of the leading political, literary and scientific figures of his day, and furnished some extraordinary anecdotes about them. I obviously considered this journal to be a major source of information for my biography. Fortunately, despite the existence of what was considered by the literary establishment to be an exemplary published edition, I decided to look at the manuscripts myself, just in case any grain of information might have been overlooked by the editor. In his preface, the editor had stated that the papers were held at the Besançon Academy, and I found their address from a book which is absolutely essential to anyone involved in research work: *The World of Learning*. This is held by most public libraries in the reference section, and lists the names and addresses of most important libraries and research institutions throughout the world. I wrote to the Academy and ascertained that the papers were to be consulted at the Municipal Library in Besançon. I contacted the library a couple of months before my planned visit, and eventually obtained permission to consult the manuscript. This is absolutely essential: researchers must always obtain permission in advance to work with any manuscript or archive material. It is advisable to explain your project, and give as much detail as possible about the kind of material you hope to consult. If you have no specific references, you may be saved a wasted journey if the library/archive does not hold what you need; many libraries are open only for certain hours or at certain times of the year – one institution where I worked in France was open just the Thursday and the Friday of the first week of every month – and many curators will also ask you to supply references or written guarantees of your probity before granting access.

Despite my forward planning, however, I arrived in Besançon on that first visit to learn that the staff had never heard of me: the chief librarian was unavailable. Fortunately, I had taken his letter with me, and after heated discussions, several hours later, the manuscripts were rather grudgingly produced.

Manuscript material should obviously be treated with a great deal of respect. Any manuscript (however seemingly mundane) is a unique document which can never be completely replaced, and other people will need to work with the document in the future. (This sort of comment ought to be unnecessary, but experience has unfortunately taught me that even some well-known and respected scholars have been guilty of careless and irresponsible treatment of precious documents.) A manuscript should never be marked or annotated in any way whatsoever. Most libraries possessing manuscript material forbid even the presence of ink or Biros (so take a good supply of pencils!). Pages must be turned carefully, and bound volumes should normally be placed on a lectern with pegs to hold pages open. If you are faced with the prospect of sifting through quantities of unclassified material, you should always replace the documents in the order in which they were found – even if it appears to be a total muddle! Finally, always cover yourself. If any document appears to he damaged or missing, inform the librarian immediately. Otherwise, you could be held responsible.

The material, when it eventually arrived, consisted of some 3000 pages (the published version covered less than 800 pages) of faded, spidery handwriting which appeared to be totally illegible. I sat there for the remaining three hours the library was open that day, attempting to find any form on that first page (or indeed, on any other!) which might have resembled a word. I was on the brink of tears. I had travelled to Besançon with very little financial assistance, done battle with some very unhelpful librarians – and I couldn't understand a word of the (nearly) 3000 pages I had come to study!

The following day I returned to the library and simply sat there, as the previous day, reading and re-reading that first page, until finally, somehow, some sort of recognition dawned – and, very slowly at first, I was away! I subsequently discovered that my reaction on seeing the manuscript for the first time was fairly standard (if perhaps exacerbated by the truly dreadful handwriting of my subject!). Most documents, particularly if written in earlier centuries (although don't forget, the advent of the typed word, even for public records, is relatively recent), can be disconcerting. But don't despair – persistence pays! Patience is definitely the most necessary virtue for working with manuscript material, be it waiting for documents to be fetched, trying to decipher unfamiliar handwriting, or sifting through enormous cardboard boxes of boring, irrelevant and usually very dusty papers. My perseverance in this case turned up a result I had certainly not expected. It transpired that the published version, which has been used as a standard work of reference by historians, is actually very different from Marmier's papers in Besançon. Dates, names, places, figures, people and sexes are muddled and wrongly transcribed. Referring to archive material, therefore, was extremely important for my work, despite the existence of a modern and acclaimed text, and illustrates the necessity of checking everything, even the work of established and respected critics.

Then, as I went on reading Marmier's words direct from his pen, an unexpected emotional tie with the subject came into play. For days and days I had been reading nothing but Marmier's private thoughts, including some very secret memories which had never been published, and had seldom, if ever, been read by anyone else, so that Marmier started to take over my own life. I read his *mémoires* by day and dreamed of him at night. I became aware that I knew him better than anyone else alive today – I was his link with the modern world. I began to feel strongly indignant on his behalf and decided that I wanted the extent of the misunderstandings surrounding him to be made public knowledge as soon as possible. In order to set that particular record straight, I resolved not to wait until documentation for the biography was complete, but to write an article about my findings as soon as possible.

A year or so later, I was working in the library and

archive of the French Academy at the Institut de France (this particular institution, incidentally, has a difficult and time-consuming procedure for gaining access: a good case to illustrate my point about writing in advance . . .) when I came across some even more interesting information. In his preface to the published edition of Marmier's journal, the editor had claimed that a certain 'Etincelle', a journalist on the *Figaro* around the turn of the century, was the daughter of either Marmier or the famous poet Victor Hugo by a certain Léonie d'Aunet. All sorts of quotations and references were given to support the assertion that the child was Marmier's. I was naturally intrigued and very keen to follow this up. Manuscript documents at the library of the Institut de France had been cited as the source for these claims. I located the relevant papers without too much trouble, although here I should perhaps add a word of warning. After gaining access to a library or archive, you should go along with as much information as possible to ease your search. If, for example, you know the exact date of birth rather than just the year, the search for a birth certificate may take minutes rather than hours, or even days. Even if you have precise references for the document you think you need, it always pays to spend a day or two familiarising yourself with the classification systems – if indeed the material is catalogued – as all libraries and archives are arranged differently. It is very hard to generalise here, but you may come across classification by date, function, establishment, personal papers, etc, depending on the kind of records you are using (eg public records, employment files, literary collections etc) and these may be catalogued on computer, card index, microfilm, or a combination of these – or possibly not at all! Don't be afraid to ask for help: everyone has to learn, although you do learn more quickly after a while. Familiarising yourself with classification systems will help you to ascertain the scope of the resources available (and don't hesitate to order documents on the off-chance – hunches will sometimes pay off), as well as making it easier to obtain the documents to be consulted. Here again, patience is of the essence, and you shouldn't be surprised if it takes you several days to obtain the material you require.

The personal papers of a certain Maxime Du Camp, an author several years younger than Marmier, but a 'crony' of his at the French Academy, contained a newspaper cutting of an obituary of Marmier written by 'Etincelle'. Beside it, Du Camp had scribbled the following: 'Etincelle is the daughter of Marmier and Madame Biard (Léonie d'Aulnet [sic for d'Aunet]), the widow of a certain Pérony [sic for Peyronny], she married the Baron Double. X Marmier told me that he didn't know if she was his daughter or Victor Hugo's.' I was fascinated by this entry, and decided to continue my investigation by attempting to find out more about this woman, supposedly the mother of Marmier's child, who had also apparently been having an affair with Hugo at the same time. Who was she? How could I, some 150 years later, discover if Etincelle really was Marmier's daughter?

After ascertaining the correct spelling of her name, I began to work my way through the standard biographies of the day, and also through the many Hugo biographies available. I was horrified to come across a plethora of misogynist comments, even in one of the most recent and most widely respected Hugo biographies. The general gist of these comments repeatedly casts Léonie into two traditional stereotype roles for women: as muse and whore. As muse, she is mentioned in the footnotes to several poems by Hugo. As whore, she is portrayed as a promiscuous and greedy, grasping woman who caused Hugo a great deal of embarrassment by being sent to prison! I undertook further research involving press records, archive material and law statutes of the day, and I slowly began to uncover a very grim tale of injustice; of a woman's suffering in a male-dominated world. (Press records, incidentally, are a rich source of information, but call for a methodical approach and a good pair of reading glasses since most newspapers nowadays are only available on microfilm. A good place to start if you are in Britain is the British Newspaper Library at Colindale.) I also uncovered first-class evidence of how history is neatly presented to justify (and indeed perpetuate) man's inhumanity to woman. The following summarises my quite extraordinary findings.

At the age of 16 or 17, Léonie d'Aunet went to live with the famous artist François Biard, who was approximately twice her age. Léonie, who was beautiful and intelligent, was rapidly accepted by Biard's friends as 'Madame Biard', although the couple did not actually marry until Léonie was pregnant. By all evidence the relationship sounds to have been, in the early stages at least, a good one.

In 1839, the famous explorer Paul Gaimard needed Biard as an official artist (a very important function, since photography had not yet been invented) on his forthcoming expedition to Spitzbergen, aboard the vessel *La Recherche*. He approached Léonie to put the proposition to Biard on his behalf, hoping thus to pre-empt Biard's possible reluctance to leave Léonie alone in Paris. But Léonie had other ideas; she responded enthusiastically to Gaimard's proposition, and guaranteed to persuade Biard to accept, on condition that she be allowed to join the expedition. In 1839 this was an extremely problematic proposition on several grounds. The area surrounding Spitzbergen was still largely undocumented territory, and one of the major aims of the expedition was to map the area, while other scientists undertook geological,

meteorological and hydrographical studies. The voyage
was a difficult and dangerous enterprise even for a seaman
of Gaimard's experience: indeed, the expeditions of the
'Commission du Nord' aboard *La Recherche* had originally
been instigated four years previously to trace the remains
of a French gunboat which was presumed to have sunk
somewhere between Iceland and Greenland. The journey
to Spitzbergen was more dangerous still, because there was
the very real risk that the ship would become frozen
into the ice. This had indeed happened to a number of
earlier expeditions. Undaunted by the physical dangers
of the voyage, a more immediate problem, so far as Léonie
was concerned, was the fact that women were strictly
forbidden on board any vessel of the French navy. But
Léonie remained adamant in her resolve to participate,
and she was eventually granted permission to board the
ship at Hammerfest, the most northerly point of civilis-
ation, with Biard. This they did on 17 July.

The official reporter of this expedition was Xavier
Marmier, which is perhaps how the rumours of his
paternity began. But a simple chronology drawn up from
the different records of the journey shows that he could
not possibly have been the father of Léonie's daughter
(quite apart from the fact that with Biard present on the
same ship, Marmier and Léonie would have had to be
extremely ingenious in engineering their meeting without
arousing his supicions!). *La Recherche* arrived back in
Hammerfest on 22 August, and the party travelled across
Lapland down to Haparanda and Stockholm. Even if
Marmier had been Léonie's lover, the child could not
have been his, since she was born in either October or
November 1840, and the Biards had arrived back in Paris
at the end of 1839: Marmier had meanwhile travelled to
Copenhagen, where he spent several months![1] It is also
most unlikely that Hugo could have been the father of this

child, since there is no suggestion at all of any affair between them at this stage.

What I found most disconcerting about this part of the 'Léonie story' was the way in which a significant number of scholars (all men!) had quite shamelessly altered or omitted dates, misquoted poems, place names and other vital pieces of information in order to prove that Marmier had been the father of the child.

Worse was to come. It also transpired that Léonie had left Biard and applied for a legal separation around April 1844, some five or six months into her second pregnancy (divorce had been abolished in 1816, and was not reinstated until 1884). In July 1845, Léonie was caught in compromising circumstances with Hugo by Biard, accompanied by the chief of police. Adultery at that time was illegal for a married woman, and Biard pressed charges. (A man could have his wife sent to prison for adultery, even if they were living apart, but adultery for the husband was permissible. A wife could not even ask for separation from her husband on the simple grounds of adultery, unless he had brought a mistress or mistresses to live in the marital home.) Léonie was sent to St. Lazare prison until the end of September, when pressure was brought to bear on Biard by the king to authorise her transfer to a convent, where she was forcibly detained for a further period. On her release, she had lost everything, including her children, whom she was now permitted to visit for just one hour a week. With no means of financial support, she now had to find a means of making a living, which was no easy task for a woman in the nineteenth century, particularly if she had a prison record. She began by publishing her record of the journey to Spitzbergen in 1854. I was curious to read this work for several reasons: first, I was obviously familiar with Marmier's official account of the expedition, and was keen to compare the two. Also, I had read so many descriptions of Léonie and so many (misogynist) comments about her life and achievements (including her writing) that I was quite determined to see something that she had actually written. The book is fascinating, and, as one might have suspected, reveals Léonie to have been a woman of tremendous courage, both physical and moral, and also a talented writer. The narrative covers not only the first major expedition to Spitzbergen (Léonie was the first woman ever to set foot there) and its physical dangers, but also communicates the awe and wonder inspired by the unexpected purity and the overwhelming might of this glacial land. A number of comments also reveal the additional difficulties encountered by the only woman on such an expedition. There is also an account of the extremely arduous journey across Lapland.

I was so moved both by the book and by all that I had discovered about Léonie, that I decided not only to write an article to set the record straight on some of the comments which continue to be made about her, and to pay a belated tribute to her life and achievements, but also to find a publisher for a new edition of the book, which had been forgotten for over a hundred years. Thanks to my research on Marmier, and the knowledge I had of the works published on the expeditions in the area, I located and purchased a number of very beautiful illustrations which had not been included in Léonie's original book. These I offered along with the text to a number of publishing houses. It was at this stage that I discovered the absolute necessity of taking steps to safeguard your work. The fact that you may have spent years following up clues and tracking down material does not give you an inalienable right to what you have discovered – archive material is in the public domain, which means that there is no copyright and the material may be published by whoever comes across it, by whatever means, without payment. I approached several publishing houses and eventually found one who was interested in the story and willing to publish the book. I was asked to supply a clean copy of the text, and an introduction outlining the life and achievements of Léonie, with particular reference to the 'Hugo affair'. The task was made difficult by a variety of factors. Firstly, Hugo's letters to Léonie, which had been held in a private collection with no public access (another real problem for the researcher: all I can say is that begging and a written assurance of acknowledgement in print *sometimes* works), had finally been published the previous month, but in a limited edition which had already sold out. The copy held by the Bibliothèque Nationale had been removed for binding. Secondly the text itself was obviously by now very rare. In order to supply a copy of it, I had to find a library which owned a copy of the book, and was prepared to allow me to photocopy it. (Many libraries, including the Bibliothèque Nationale, categorically refuse to allow any book over a hundred years old to be photocopied.)

I prepared my introduction and, by great good fortune, I managed to photocopy the text in London. The whole lot was sent to the publisher on time. At first, I heard nothing, other than that the photocopy was not clear enough for the laser scanner. I found a photocopy shop with a superior machine, and tried again, and this time the copies were clear enough for the scanner.

I was rather disturbed to hear nothing for about two months after this. The delay, it transpired, had been caused by the publisher rewriting my introduction. I was unhappy with the changes they had made, so by dint of argument, I came to agree an introduction with the publishers which, from my point of view, was just about acceptable. The final version as it now appears in published form does not contain any blatant errors of fact, but does, however, omit a great deal of important material I would have liked to have seen included and, in my opinion, is written in very poor French.

I learned that the book had eventually been published from a friend who saw an article about it in a newspaper. My name appeared in very small letters on the back of the cover, on the second title page, and at the end of the rewritten introduction which still makes me squirm with embarrassment. Financially, I received a small advance which went nowhere near covering the final cost of my work and my expenses.

I have finished my piece on archive work with this unhappy tale in the hope that it may serve as a salutary lesson. There are steps which can be taken to protect both your work, and your rights, although where archive material is concerned this is always tricky. If you suspect that your work could become a commercial success, then it is probably worthwhile making contact with a literary agent, who will be able to negotiate on your behalf; if possible, try to find your agent through personal recommendation (see also Dorothy Lumley's chapter). If you do not think your work is liable to make much money, then many agents might not be interested in helping. If you do find yourself seeking a publisher on your own, then it is obviously important to exercise caution when deciding which houses to approach. It is always useful to check out what they have published in the past and, if possible, it is a good idea to try to talk with authors who have worked with them. Another very important precaution is to refuse to hand over any material until you have a contract in your hand. Even if a contract is promised, it is advisable to wait until you actually receive it. In order to protect your integrity (ie to prevent the publisher rewriting your findings and presenting them in a manner you find unacceptable) you can insist on a clause in the contract stipulating that nothing will be published without your express permission. This should include any corrections made at proof stage. You can also insist that provisions are made concerning, for example, where your name appears, and in what format, as well as all the financial arrangements. If you have an agent, s/he should be able to help you through all this; if not, and you have a serious concern about any detail, it could be worth taking legal advice: although this can prove expensive, it could turn out to be money well spent in the long term (see also Lynettte Owen's chapter).

Finally, it is only fair to say that although my experience shows clearly that discretion should be exercised in dealings with publishers if you have never worked with them before, it would be wrong to suggest that those particular publishers are in any way representative: the majority of houses I have subsequently worked with have been perfectly professional, competent and correct in all their dealings.

Notes

1 Full details of all these references can be found in my article 'Léonie d'Aunet (1820–79) in the shade of Victor Hugo: talent hidden by sex', *Studi Francesi*, CIX, 1993, pp. 31–46.

ORGANISATION

Planning to write
Judith Baxter

At about 8.30 am I start looking at the house because the housekeeper arrives at nine and I'm too well brought up to offer a house in disarray, so I straighten up before she comes in . . . My secretary also comes in at nine and that's when real life begins. She says, 'Ms Angelou, you've got to sign this, send that, agree to that, deny this . . .' and I say, 'Mrs Garris, I will talk to you in an hour.'

At ten, I deal with my correspondence . . .

'A Life in the Day of Maya Angelou', *The Sunday Times*

In my eternal quest for an organised life as a writer, I have often marvelled at the seamless ease and effortless sense of order in the lives of those writers interviewed for *The Sunday Times* feature. The articles exude an aura of well-being, as if life has arranged itself around the writer, ready to obey commands, supply comforts, and reorganise itself at the drop of a hat. 'A Life in the Day of . . .' suggests to me a pattern for each day which is somehow predetermined as if some divine figure has given her blessing on the writer's life. Drinking an orange juice at 6 am has as much significance in that overall pattern as sending a manuscript off to a publisher at the end of the day. In Maya Angelou's case, the surface order of each day may be a vital antidote to her own writing which presents so colourfully the wonderful diversity and chaos of people's lives.

Suppose a *Sunday Times* journalist were to interview me? We all have our dreams. Would I be able to marshal my day into a life which sounded as if it has meaning, coherence and purpose? Would I be able to supply times, like a British Rail timetable, proving that my daily life has been structured into a sequence of achievements all destined to further my writing career? Only a brief scan over the inchoate mass of my life: the multiple roles of wife, mother, daughter, housekeeper, part-time lecturer, writer, editor, neighbour, friend; the frenzied childcare arrangements; the dashing between workplace and home; the forgotten dental appointments, tell me otherwise. Surely it would be impossible to render such an order over my life that gave it any sense of typicality, mission, and, least of all, set an example to others?

One answer to this would be: yes, I could do it, and so could you. The reason for this is simply that our ability to use narrative as a means of organising and making sense of our experiences, is one of the most powerful tools we have. Story-making, whether it be through recounting dreams, telling anecdotes, exchanging gossip, cracking jokes, or perhaps keeping a diary, is a fundamental way of attributing logic, sense, order and importance to our lives.

Another answer would be: no, I couldn't do it. If we make even the most simple attempt to deconstruct the *Sunday Times* feature, it becomes obvious that only writers who have 'made it' get invited to contribute their daily life stories. 'Making it' does indeed confer a charmed life upon the writer: money can buy you space, time and support. The mundane routines: cleaning the house, doing the ironing, picking the children up from school, making meals, paying bills – the stuff of ordinary people's lives – can slip invisibly into the background when you can afford to write for your living, and live for your writing. I remember reading an article in the late 1980s on the professional and married lives of Tom and Miriam Stoppard – they had his and her studies, telephones and secretaries, but shared domestic staff. For the rest of us, however, organising our lives as a writer, and organising our material into finished pieces, are challenges just as great as the more 'creative' tasks – whether gaining inspiration to write, finding our 'voice', or expressing our ideas; and the more 'technical' tasks, say, of finding a publisher. Overcoming the many organisational hurdles is essential to get going as a writer. Ironically, though, in the Catch 22 business of becoming a writer – unless you can learn to be organised, you may never earn the means to be organised.

1 Becoming a writer

In 1986, I was working as a Head of English in a Hampshire sixth-form college when I became pregnant with my first child. After my daughter was born, I decided for various reasons not to go back, but to 'devote myself to motherhood'. Secretly I was relieved to have escaped the treadmill of the daily career grind. But once I had surfaced from the first months of breast-feeding, I knew that I wanted to make something of the expertise I had left behind. The idea came to me to write a coursebook for a readership which was *not* being catered for at that time by educational publishers. I knew this because, as a head of department, I had searched in vain for a suitable course-book and none was available. Like many other teachers, I had been forced to devise a year's course of material, partly by myself and partly with my colleagues.

So, I knew that I had all the raw material, and I knew that I had a good idea. The challenge was to get a publisher interested, preferably *before* writing the book. I decided to send a proposal to every significant educational publisher. By blitzing them in this way, I was lucky enough to get four or five editors eager to pursue the idea further. I submitted a sample chapter to each of these editors, and began to work with the editor who first responded positively. There was a lot of work to be done before we moved to contracts: criticisms of my sample chapter from the editor, and later from the 'readers' – experts who read and review the sample material and either recommend or reject it – to which I had to respond, but this, effectively, was the start of my writing career.

Writing one book successfully usually leads to writing others. I have never had to submit another proposal. By working closely with one publisher, I have been able to choose what I write, and indeed help to determine the kinds of books that are used in schools and colleges. Each successive year, I have taken on more writing projects and a series editorship. None of this has as yet made me financially self-sufficient, or given me the means to organise my life like the *Sunday Times* feature. What I have learnt is that there is a delicate balance to be achieved between self-disciplining strategies which order and regulate the writing you do; and ways of letting go, relaxing, and switching between roles without stress.

2 Conditions for writing

My life is slightly mad . . . after washing out bedpans and coping with the measled ones I rush . . . and minister to Christian . . . and when I have turned him upside down, pinned his nappy on wrong . . . I hurl him into his cot and find Flavia wanting to put on a party frock . . . I chuck her a doll to play with and then rush to the privacy of a room alone and hammer upon my typewriter at *Frenchman's Creek*, my new book, and I am lucky if I get a page written.

Daphne du Maurier, letter to Grace Browning

Despite the whirlwind sense of anarchy in Daphne du Maurier's description of her day, there is still a sense that the manic energy she displays in fending off her children's needs, might have transmuted into an imaginative power when she wrote her novel.

For other writers, and certainly for those of us who are writing more 'technical' books, it is probable that if you want to feel organised in your approach to writing, then you will need some sense of order and organisation in your own life. If everything is swirling in chaos around you, it is unlikely that you will find the sense of calm discipline to apply yourself to the job. From my experience there are several factors which might encourage that peace of mind.

Time

First, it can be helpful to draw up a long-term timetable which charts the time you have available to produce your manuscript. The determining factor may be a deadline negotiated with your editor or publisher. Make sure that this deadline is realistic, and that you really have enough time to do the work. I leave at least four months for my coursebooks; authors of handbooks, health or political books tell me that realistic deadlines for them are nine months to a year and sometimes more. This time span might then be divided up so that you aim to complete a section, or chapter, each month or each fortnight. Leave plenty of time before submission for reading through and checking.

Secondly, it is a good idea to allocate and safeguard

writing time each week. As a mother in paid employment, I am a firm believer in protected time – that is, set time on given days each week when I know I will do my writing. Florence Nightingale once said, 'Women never have half an hour they can call their own', and so often there is a sense that with a family, there are always more 'important' things to do. As a way of resisting this, I decided, when my daughter was a few months old, to place her with a childminder for three hours, twice a week. Unlike my friends' babies, Katharine was a 'crying baby' and at times it practically drove me mad. There was no way she would have cooed, played, chortled and napped on her own while I got on with my work. So I used my Child Allowance to pay the childminder's fees, and saw it as an investment in my own future. Over the following months, it was during this time, and this time alone, that I wrote my first book.

If you have no partner and no children, your time may be more flexibly yours to control. But in either case, it can be crucial that you set aside blocks of time for your work. Too often people, especially women, who work from home are considered to be available to all callers. It can be important to make it clear from the outset to friends, neighbours and family that during these hours you are not to be disturbed except in the direst emergency.

Environment

Whenever you read about writers describing how they write, they often repeat Virginia Woolf's refrain, 'a woman must have money and a room of her own if she is to write fiction.' While there are famous cases of writers with very few resources who have published masterpieces, there is a lot of truth in Woolf's words and the author's environment can be very important.

The ideal is a study with a door which shuts the world out and preferably locks; a room with a view for idle contemplation; a large desk with a word-processor and perhaps a telephone on it but still leaving space for making notes; a filing cabinet with all your materials for your book carefully catalogued; bookcases providing dictionaries and an instant source of references; a room heater if it turns cold, and maybe a fan in summer.

The reality will probably be your kitchen or dining-room table, a meeting point for family or friends who barrage you with requests; a view of a neighbour's garage wall; an ageing Amstrad that groans when you switch it on; a telephone that rings for someone else or with non-work demands; a pile of unsorted papers and bills on a shelf; a rack of motley books competing with videos and CDs; heating that you can only afford to switch on for an hour after tea.

So how do you create an environment fit to write in? If possible, it is a good idea to choose a room which is not being used at that time of day, and aim to do all your writing in that same space, so that it becomes a part of your writing practice. If home is impossible, consider a space away from the madding crowd – perhaps in a university or city library.

Freeing the mind

You are likely only to be able to concentrate on your writing and organise your thoughts clearly, if you come to your work with a fresh, uncluttered and relaxed state of mind. Part of this is to do with having time and physical space, without noise and interruption; the other part is to do with psychological space.

Imagine the brain is divided into two halves: the left hemisphere responsible for the logical, rational and organisational aspects of your thinking; and the right hemisphere for the more intuitive, imaginative, and creative aspects. For the left half to function properly, it is necessary to release the recuperative powers of the right; for the right side to function, you need to switch off the controlling and often dominating role of the left. To write well, both left and right sides should be working together, reciprocally and harmoniously.

Although there is physiological evidence for the hemispherical functions of the brain as I've described, I find it much more valuable as an analogy. So, my view is that 'writer's block', that sense of not being able to get started, is much to do with the inhibiting control of the logical left-side – often forced into dominance in our lives by the need constantly to control sources of stress. Until we release this, and let the right side flourish, then it will be difficult to think creatively, or indeed to write at all.

So how is it possible to achieve that sense of balance for writing? One way is to try to empty the mind of clutter before writing. Here are some fairly obvious ideas which have worked for me:

- structured breaks
- going for a walk and not thinking
- taking some form of leisurely exercise
- reading a newspaper, a book, something light
- doing paper-shuffling activities, mildly useful
- gaze out of the window for half an hour and allow your mind to go blank
- do a practical but non-thinking activity
- visit/see/phone someone

When you see that 'time out' is as necessary to productive writing as time spent at the word processor, that sense of frustration at 'wasting time' may be considerably eased.

3 A conceptual framework

> For the next six or seven years, I wrestled with structure, accumulating a great heap of manuscripts under my bed, until I finally met someone who gave me a formula I could work to. I think a lot of people are put off for life by the difficulty of organising material; I know I might never have had the confidence to continue unless someone had stepped in to help.
> Emma Tennant, *Delighting the Heart*

Once time has been created, space found, you know what you are going to write about, feel ready and perhaps have collected some of the data, it is time to start thinking about structuring your material.

Most non-fiction books, and especially those whose task is to inform or teach its readership, will have to be driven by a conceptual framework – a theoretical rationale for the approaches and material offered. This framework is likely to be new, and rather different from that of other authors in your field. Therefore it is important to do two things:

— make very explicit to yourself exactly what your conceptual framework is
— research those in rival publications and articulate how your approach differs

Your conceptual framework could operate on two levels:

1 As a set of principles and outcomes

These should represent a basis of expertise in your given subject, suggesting both what is valuable and important about the framework you have adopted (the principles), and what you hope your book will achieve in terms of benefits, or outcomes for the reader.

In the case of my school coursebook, *English for GCSE: A Course for Further Education*, an example of my principles (summarised) were these:

- an awareness of the characteristics and needs of the young adult student and a sense of their preparation for entry into adulthood
- importance of student-centred (rather than teacher-led) learning
- the interrelatedness and integration of the four language modes: speaking, listening, reading and writing in learning English
- a belief in learning as a developmental process from exploration of an initial idea, through to oral or written performance

The outcomes or benefits to the reader should be linked very closely to the principles you have articulated. An example of *one* possible outcome connected to the final item on the list above might read:

- the student is able to explore an initial idea in some depth, by using a range of language activities: role play, discussion, games, creative writing

2 As a practical model

Your principles can translate into a workable model offering a mechanism for achieving your outcomes. This model could provide the basis for a plan of the structure of your book, dividing it into a sequence of discrete sections. It is almost impossible to generalise about how to plan a book, but if your material is structured in such a way that it answers the following questions, then you will have achieved focus, direction and clarity:

What? What is the book/chapter/section about?
Who? Who is it aimed at?
Why? Why is it important?
How? How will readers use it?
When? When should they go about it/how long should they take?

For *English for GCSE* I developed a very simple model that provided the basic floorplan for each chapter in the book. I chose a different theme (the 'What') as the stimulus and focus of study for each chapter, such as the family, love, emnity, danger, injustice, and so on. Each chapter then followed an identical pattern (the 'How)', where students were guided through four stages of learning – reading a selection of stimulus materials; exploring these materials through various oral activities; learning particular study skills in order to produce a piece of work; and finally, writing and presenting that piece of work to a specified audience (see page 88):

It can be very important to spend time at this early planning stage, playing with ideas on paper and just mulling things over. Once you have a plan you are satisfied with, the business of writing your book will appear manageable and achievable because you have a clear model to work to.

stages of learning	1	2	3	4
	examples of reading	ways to explore	ways to learn & practice	ways to write & perform
student activities	short stories	role play	note taking	stories/poems/plays
	poems	research	essay planning	dramatic performances
	articles	discussion	rehearsing	essays/debates/speeches
	playscripts	games	drafting a story	articles/letters/leaflets

4 The writing process

Different writers have different strategies for the best way to get the manuscript actually written. This is what works best for me: first I determine roughly how much I hope to achieve during a single writing session, aiming fairly high. Then I try to write or type swiftly and continuously, without agonising over the expression of each sentence. I don't worry about whether I am writing entirely without style, grace or accuracy. I just write, and cover the page. When I have finished, I leave it. I take a breather – by walking the dog; picking up the children; making the tea; watching TV; or going to bed. Later, or the next day, I take a look at what I have written. *Now* is the time to scrutinise it.

This mix of sustained periods of concentrated writing, taking breaks, then returning to look over what I have written works very well for me. This balance of the left/

right functions of the mind, helps me to experience writing as, on occasions, productive bursts of energy, combined with calmer periods of reflection and review.

5 Presenting material

I believe that there are at least six principles governing good presentation of material. If I were to turn to any page of my manuscript, I would expect it to observe the following checklist:

1. Clarity	— does the material answer the six questions (What? Who? Why? How? When/Where? on page 87)
	— does the layout convey the broad nature of the subject matter at a glance?
2. Order	— has each section been presented in an orderly and logical way?
	— have I made good use of headings and sub-headings to divide sections and sub-sections?
	— have I made links and connections between one section and the next?
	— have I made use of numbered (or bulleted) points where there is a list of points or questions to be made?
3. Variety	— is each page visually appealing?
	— is there a good mix of text, and, if appropriate, illustrations and graphics and white space?
	— is there variety in the design and layout of each page?

4. Consistency	— if I am presenting an argument or case through the book, is this presented and developed consistently?
	— are headings, labels, linguistic terminology, layout, the way I am addressing the reader, all used in a consistent way throughout?
5. Simplicity	— am I using language simply, in such a way that it clarifies and explains, rather than obscures, complicates and confuses?
	— am I keeping instructions concise and straightforward?
	— am I presenting material in a direct, clear, and simple way?
6. Reader awareness	— have I maintained a sense of the kind of reader I am addressing at all times as I write?
	— is my use of subject matter, language, illustrations (if any), and layout appropriate to the age and character of that readership?

Such a checklist helps me to keep certain criteria in my head as I progress and also when I come to look over or review my work. However, nothing beats the power of intuition. If I feel that something looks wrong; fails to make sense; or lacks conviction, I change it.

6 Checking material

The moment of finishing the first draft of a manuscript can be an exhilarating and liberating experience. A little like leaving the exam room, you feel like shouting with joy, and doing something crazy; you don't care what the examiner thinks of the script for the time being – the exam is over.

Then reality dawns, the script must be read, a mark must be given, a future depends on it, and suddenly life sobers up. The moment I know other people must read my manuscript, I break out in a cold sweat. They can read it, sure, but please, please don't criticise it!

This, of course, is the stage when the most productive work on a manuscript is likely to happen. As much as I dread it, I know that my own writing will benefit vastly from the viewpoints of a range of critics. At the same time I know I must be prepared to defend what I believe to be valuable. Generally, I expect my manuscript to be subject to the following stages of scrutiny:

1. **Personal scrutiny**: when I have completed the first draft (which I will have already reviewed at the end of each chapter or stage) I read the whole thing through, being merciless in my self-criticism. I'm aware that if I'm not merciless, others will be. I'm always prepared to spend up to a month on making changes.

2. **Scrutiny of a friend**: sometimes I ask someone I trust to read it through as well – my partner, a close friend, or a colleague at work. They need have no special qualifications! A lay-person with a 'common sense' view often spots inconsistencies and poor expression more easily than 'an expert'.

3. **Scrutiny by my intended readership**: nowadays it's essential that all 'technical' material is trialled with a sample group from the target audience, and this can be a good idea for all non-fiction. Even if I have previously used the material from my books as teaching material, I

still 'try out' the book's material with my intended readership. As a one-time teacher of school students this was easy in the past; now, as a university lecturer, I persuade my colleagues in schools to trial the material for me.

4. **Editorial scrutiny**: most editors of publishing houses send manuscripts out to 'readers' for scrutiny – experts in the field of the book who will write reports on the work, and advise changes. Their reports are likely to be astute, direct, positively critical and to offer constructive suggestions for revisions.

If you manage to survive this trial by criticism, you will have passed the exam, but may not feel quite so euphoric as when you believed you had first 'finished'! With most books, however, the submission of a completed manuscript to the publisher means the start of a *new* stage – one of collaborative authorship. Suddenly the manuscript is no longer your own as designers, illustrators, editors, marketing and sales representatives all move in to discuss the design and 'packaging' of your book. How much you are involved in this depends on the type of book and publisher. In some cases, many months of work may follow as you discuss technical matters like the use of illustrations, the layout of pages, and suitable titles; or you agree to run workshops at conferences, give presentations to sales reps, and help with copies for publicity brochures.

Last word

> Writing is . . . difficult for any male not born into a class that breeds confidence. Almost impossible for a girl, a woman.
> Tillie Olsen, *Silences*

What connects the writing of any book – fiction or non-fiction – is the sheer surprise that it is possible to do at all. Consider how much it seems to take – time, space, money, an interested publisher, a developing ability in your craft, a vision, and, immeasurably more important than all this, a store of belief in yourself that what you have to say is valuable and worthwhile, and can withstand the criticisms of others.

Books like *Instead of Full Stops* may turn the impossible into the possible: by reading other women's stories, and by writing oneself, we all contribute to the new 'class' of women now writing in *all* genres, who provide the inspiration and example for women in the future.

Putting practice on paper
Gerrilyn Smith

I write books based on my own professional experience, and my first consideration is always how to approach my material in a way that reflects what I want to say and how I want to say it. Many other women who write books based on professional experience are faced with the same dilemma, since most professions have both journals and publications that suggest a way of writing about professional experience that may seem alien to women. The style is often very detached and intellectually removed from the actual experiences being described. Because I do not think about my work as a clinical psychologist in that way, I don't like writing about it in that way. I also want to reach a wider audience not just my fellow (sic) colleagues.

I believe that it is essential to choose a style that fits with your professional practice or context and also to ensure that, whatever the nature of the book, you will be happy with the finished product, because a book is a testament to what you believe you practice. I no longer feel that my manuscript must be 'perfect' before submitting it for publication and this has been extremely liberating. I view my written work as thinking aloud – the finished product doesn't capture forever what I feel about the subject. It is a punctuation mark in my intellectual life. This perspective enables me to play with ideas and not feel burdened by the permanent record a publication makes of my thoughts.

Writing should be enjoyable and the writer's pleasure should be conveyed to the reader.

What do you want to say and who do you want to say it to?

As Judith Baxter's chapter has demonstrated, knowing who you are writing for and why you are writing is an essential first step along the way to creating a written record of your current thinking. At the beginning, you are often writing for yourself, but in most non-fiction work the target audience must, by the end of the process, have set the tone and voice for your piece. Sometimes as the project gets underway, I have found that the voice has changed and that I am writing to a different audience. This change in voice may be appropriate and the piece may come together much better when written for a different audience than the one envisaged at the outset.

Once I have a completed piece, I always need to read it with the target audience in mind and correct any portions where I may have drifted into addressing someone else, either by deleting those passages completely, collecting them together into a new section or by changing the voice so that the whole piece is consistently addressed to the same audience.

Before I write anything for publication, from a short article to a whole book, I try to focus on what it is I want to say. I look for an organising principle or belief about my subject matter that can then be conveyed to my audience. This organising principle should be able to bring all of the material together and help shape what I will include and exclude along the way.

I think readers like to read something that has a clear point of view even if they do not necessarily agree with it. Encouraging your audience to follow the development of your ideas is part of engaging them in the process of a book so that by the end, they can arrive at their own conclusions regarding what you have said.

My writing style is designed to be very close to my speaking style because I want to create an immediacy with the readers of my piece. I want to be clear so that they can follow what I am thinking. I also want to make my professional experience and thinking accessible to them. Sometimes when I am experiencing difficulties with a certain passage or portion of my work I will read it out loud to get a better sense of what it is I am trying to say.

Using outlines

Like many of the other contributors to this volume, I work to an outline. This provides a skeleton for your writing as well as section headings or chapters. I find that sitting down and spending some time working on an outline is invaluable when it comes to writing up the piece as it helps to direct where I am going, keeps me on target for what it is I want to say and gives me something to assess myself against when I have finished.

The outline also helps direct me to appropriate material that supports my thesis or point of view. Once I have my outline I can begin to build up material that can be matched to its topic headings. When I have interviewed people for the piece or want to use direct quotes, I find it useful to highlight or mark out those portions I wish to use. These quotes should be selected because they illustrate an important point rather than make the point for you. I keep the material in section headings even after I have completed a draft because I sometimes find that the quote I have used isn't appropriate when the piece is finished and that there is a better quote from my original collection.

(For more advice on using quotes, see Alex Bennion's chapter.)

Having a range of background material is important. This can include direct interview material, research articles, other texts as well as references in newspapers or the media. Once the writing starts, it is usual to become attuned to the issue and start to notice material that previously you would not have. For example in between the second and third draft of this chapter, I came across an article written in *The Psychologist*[1] which made some useful points about productive writing. It often proves very valuable to collect any material you may come across and keep it in the folder or filing system you have devised for your work. If you find something that might be interesting or relate to a current writing project, such as my discovery of the reference in *The Psychologist*, it is important to mark where you got it from – chasing up serendipitous references later on can be especially difficult.

I usually write without direct quotes the first time round and then insert examples once I have a better idea of the finished piece. When I am using academic references, I find it easier just to insert a shorthand note to myself to remind me to get the full reference later (usually the author's name and year of publication). In a long piece with many academic references I collect the full references separately as I go along so that I can put them quickly in to the text or notes and references section at the end of the writing process when I am ready to submit.

In drawing up an outline, I find points or major themes rather than written material are most helpful. Sometimes I write an introduction which summarises what it is I want to say and how I intend to say it, coupled with a detailed outline of the structure of the book. This is often what I send to a publisher in the first instance. The introduction gives them an idea about my writing style and the outline shows them how I plan to develop my ideas. It needs to be interesting and to be saying something that hasn't already been said. I always include a rationale as to why the book needs to be written or the subject addressed in the manner I am suggesting.

As the other contributors point out, the outline usually breaks the writing task down in to manageable bits. Each of the bits should be essential in helping to lead the reader through the topic so that she too can arrive at a similar understanding. Working in sections also helps to organise the work around themes and issues. You can collect any material relevant to a particular section. You can make notes to yourself about thoughts or ideas relating to the section and check that you have mentioned them as you begin to write up the piece.

In my case, the outline starts off being very stark and gradually becomes more detailed and filled in until finally the outline *becomes* the written piece. The outline is often modified and elaborated upon as the author gets into the writing of the book.

It is useful to keep outlines and written notes because when you have produced your final draft you may want to read it against what you originally intended to do and ensure that important points have been covered. It doesn't matter first time around what exactly gets written down as the editing process will streamline and sometimes reshape a piece. In the first instance it is important to develop a flow of writing which can be tidied up later.

I tend to work in sequential order through the outline as each chapter often builds on from the previous one, although not all books will be structured like this. Sometimes it will become clear that the order of the chapters needs to be changed because they do not flow one on to the other, or that the book has, say, two distinct sections: one which deals with an overview of the subject and one which deals with practical applications or suggestions. This is often not evident at the outset.

In writing non-fiction, there is always in the first draft more material to be excluded than included. Often this is because certain points are inevitably repeated in several places, the material is better placed somewhere else or the examples or material have already successfully been incorporated into the text and the added support of what someone else has said or an extra example to back up the point isn't needed any more. It is painful, but important, to be very selective about the material you do decide to include (see also Alex Bennion's chapter).

The writing process

I tend to write at times when I can be alone for a couple of hours, which for women with children often means late at night or very early in the morning. Like Judith Baxter, I find it absolutely essential to set aside time to do my writing, including the planning and preparation stage. Research suggests that a brief daily regime produces more and better writing than long hauls[2] and this is certainly the case for me. Writing in a comfortable place away from distractions and disruptions is also crucial in my case, although as my four-year-old climbs up the stairs to ask my opinion about something *again*, I try to imagine where this place with no disruptions and distractions might be!

For long pieces like books, you obviously need longer periods of time to work because it is more difficult to stop and start than with a shorter piece. It takes longer to pick up the train of thought or themes you were developing, especially at the beginning when the shape of the book is still very fluid. However, I find that once I have devised a basic structure and managed to develop an outline with chapter headings, I can focus on chapters at a time and get away with smaller chunks of working time.

The first draft is always the hardest. In a way this is because it is often impossible to know what the finished piece is going to look like at this stage. The first draft should therefore be over-inclusive so that redundant material can be edited out and material that will become the main focus can be sharpened up.

I always expect to write at least three drafts. The first I print up and edit myself. The second I usually send for comments, and I write the third after the comments have been returned. I print up copies of each draft in different coloured paper. This helps in the editing process because I can ascertain immediately which draft the editor and I are working from.

Having time in between each draft helps because it gives you the distance you need to assess your material more critically and to be able to cut those bits that you may really like, but are not relevant to the book.

Word processors have transformed the writing process for me. I used to write in pencil so I could erase and rewrite. I also press very hard when I write, especially when I am concentrating or I am very connected to what I am writing, as if the pressure of my pencil could somehow convey the urgency or the passion of my words directly to the reader. Not surprisingly I used to develop writer's cramp and my writing sessions were limited to how long my wrist or fingers could bear to grip the pencil.

Technology has changed all that. Now I write directly on to the machine but often edit drafts from hard copy. I still find it useful to see the whole piece when editing, especially with something as long as a book, and using my computer doesn't allow that. I keep each chapter as a separate file on my word processor so I can work on smaller sections without having to enter the whole document every time I want to do something.

I cut and paste my hard copy and then go back to the machine. I always keep copies of my work in the event of disaster. I can still remember the sick feeling that grabbed me when I came into work to discover my portable machine sitting in water from a flood the night before. The first thought that ran through my head was that the whole of my book was on that machine. The idea that it might be lost made me feel nauseous. Thankfully I had two copies on disks both kept in different places – one for home and one to roam, as my mother told me – as well as the most recent hard copy of the current draft.

The introduction is often the most difficult to write as it outlines the main issues and the themes the book is hoping to develop. Almost certainly it will be radically altered once the project has been completed. So I may write it *first*, to get started, but I edit it *last*. The main points may remain the same but the emphasis or order in which they have been developed may have altered dramatically.

I usually have a working title which encapsulates for me the essence of what I am doing. This rarely ends up being the actual title because it is often too cryptic to be used. It is meaningful to me but not to others. Because it captures my imagination, I ask my editors to leave it alone until I have finished the book by which time I, too, can see the book has become more than my idea and needs its own name.

My last two books had working titles of *In Search of Charmed Loops* and *Immaculate Deception*. Both very intriguing but really not very clear regarding what the books were about. They became *Systemic Approaches to Training in Child Protection* and *The Protector's Handbook: Reducing the Risk of Child Sexual Abuse and Helping Children*

Recover. While fiction may hold such enticing titles, most non-fiction books, and especially those about professional experience, need to convey clearly to potential readers what they are about.

In earlier drafts, I don't worry so much about exact references which I will chase up later. I will note something in the text to remind me of the reference. I often also make a note of an issue I would like to develop in the text but for some reason can't do at the time. The next time I read the draft I will be reminded and develop it at that time. In this way I keep track of ideas as they come, as sometimes they can be fleeting. (For detailed advice on how to use notes, see Alex Bennion's chapter.)

Towards the end of writing the book, you may want to check that the examples you have used are representative, both in terms of gender and race for instance. You may find that there are no or too few examples of black people or that all the examples are about girls. Unless you have specifically chosen to focus your piece in this way, you may want to comment in your introduction on why the pool of examples you have used is limited or you may wish to use other examples to balance out the range you have provided.

Details such as spelling, punctuation, layout are all finishing details, although I do confess to times when I become obsessively side-tracked, ensuring that there are two spaces after each full stop and so on. This is usually a sign of writer's block.

Working to a deadline is stressful. As it approaches, the planning and preparation you put in earlier will pay dividends. You can then check your written work to the original plan and more easily focus your writing on those aspects of the plan that you have not yet even drafted rather than waste precious time polishing up pieces that have been at least written albeit in an early form.

Managing your editor

Editors vary tremendously in the amount of help/interference they give. Some make no comments at all and the book/chapter/article goes in virtually as you have submitted it. This is a relatively painless procedure. Others, on the whole more conscientious ones, will make suggestions about the piece that should sharpen it up and hopefully make it fit together either as a complete work as in the case of a book, or in relation to other pieces when it is an edited collection of chapters.

It is important to try and think of the suggestions editors make as helpful. If you view the experience as an interactive one and the comments as feedback, you as the writer can feel less devastated. If you know how you respond to critical comments, it may be helpful to give your editor some hints on how to manage the feedback in a way that continues to inspire you rather than leave you feeling defeated and deflated. On long pieces of work, such as a book, I sometimes submit portions so that the editor has a feel for the piece before she receives the completed work. In this situation, I prefer to have only very general comments. Clearly if there is a major problem such as the tone is completely wrong or the thesis is unsustainable, this needs to be picked up early. For writers who are writing without the help of editors, it may be useful to enlist the help of colleagues or friends as critical readers to your piece.

The balance of positive encouraging comments should ideally outweigh the negative. The editor or critical reader should facilitate the writer in their task of writing the piece without implying that they could do it better.

The most depressing feedback occurs when editors are what I would describe as high-handed or insensitive to how much time and effort you have put in to the writing to get this far. For example I received one manuscript with feedback that started off 'This piece is badly in need of rewriting . . .'. After seeing this comment, I put the whole article to one side, didn't go on to read the rest of the comments and fretted over the feedback for days.

After very critical feedback, it can be helpful to put the book or piece of writing away for a while. Allowing yourself to recover and reflect on the comments often enables you to continue and finish the piece. Remember too that your editor wants the end product to be a success so the comments are made with the best possible intentions. It can also be useful to let your editor know how you felt about her comments as this can sometimes clear the air for you to get on with some productive writing rather than stewing on negative or critical feedback.

It is important that the book meets both your requirements as the author and those of your editor. Don't be frightened to argue to keep something in the book. It may be that you have not expressed the point clearly enough in writing. It is also important for you as the author to know the timetable for your publication. Often you have submitted your draft and then hear nothing for months. All of a sudden it is returned to you with comments and a request that you turn these around in a very short space of time because of a publishing deadline. I confess to this being my absolute pet peeve!

My advice about managing your editor, is to engage in dialogue with them. If there is more than one editor, it may be useful to ascertain which one you will work with as multiple editors can give conflicting feedback which is confusing and often unhelpful. Give them feedback on their feedback. If you appreciate their positive comments let them know how important it is to you that they believe in your work and that they think you are doing a good job. If you think they have been unhelpfully critical, raise this with them. Having a dialogue with your editor will make it easier for the more difficult times ahead, when deadlines are pressing and you have to bring the book into its final pre-publication shape.

Once you have finished with the writing of the book, the rest of the process to publication is usually much easier. The arrival of proofs signals the end of the project is nigh. It is amazing to see the book in proof. All those sheets neatly compacted down to small type and blocked out makes it look very grown-up for something that hasn't officially seen the light of day. By this stage, I am so familiar with the material, it is often very difficult for me to really read what I have written. However, by the time it is published I can approach the book as the *reader* not the *writer*. I am frequently shocked to read what I have written and almost cannot believe that I did indeed write it.

When the book is finally published, it feels as if it doesn't belong to me at all. It becomes something different and detached. In an odd way what now happens to the book never really bothers me. Usually I am already on to writing something else. I don't experience any guilt about abandoning my creations at this stage. After all, if I have done my job well, the book should be able to speak for itself!

Notes

1 Griffiths, Mark, 'Productive Writing in the Education System', *The Psychologist*, 1994, Vol 7, No 10, pp. 460–462.
2 *Ibid.*

WRITING

Writing non-fiction
Rebecca Abrams

The unmistakeable sign that I am about to embark on any sizeable piece of writing is that the house gets tidied, the car gets serviced, the leaking tap gets fixed, awkward correspondence gets attended to, and usually at least one cake gets baked. Without fail, an apparently unrelated flurry of activity is unleashed by the prospect that very soon I must sit down and start to write. Perhaps this is a peculiarly female affliction, reflecting some suppressed residue of guilt about neglecting domestic responsibilities in order to indulge 'selfish' creative urges. Or perhaps it just highlights the reality of conflicting demands and limited time, (after all, *somebody* has to think about supper). But the urge to do something else, anything else, cannot be wholly attributed to cultural or practical pressures; it seems to be, at least in part, intrinsic to the writing process itself.

My mother, herself familiar with the symptoms of writing, rang last night and inquired innocently, 'Have you started your chapter yet?' 'Well, no,' I replied, 'not quite.' 'Ah,' she murmured knowingly, 'so you're still turning round.' It took me a while to understand what she meant, but thinking about it later the analogy seemed perfect: the process of preparing oneself to write is exactly like that of a dog wheeling about in its basket before finally settling itself down. Some people accomplish this wheeling quickly and unobtrusively, others do so with considerable expenditure of time and energy. The former tend to be scathing of the latter, regarding them as ill-disciplined and unprofessional, while the latter just long to be like the former. As far as I can tell, no writer entirely escapes the wheeling process. It may only require the effort of selecting a preferred pen or putting on a certain piece of music, but whatever form it takes, some degree of preparation, some kind of pre-writing ritual seems a necessary and indispensable part of the writing process, a way of metaphorically and literally clearing a space in which the writing can take place.

There is, of course, a fine line to be drawn between clearing space and simply putting off the 'nauseous process', as Rebecca West described writing; what seems certain is that writing, particularly starting writing, is a fragile, nervy business requiring certain conditions which will vary with the individual writer and which can easily be destroyed by external events. With the possible exception of full-time journalists, the majority of writers need a sense of safe, quiet, inviolable space before they can let go of the outside world and begin to write. Wheeling about one's symbolic basket is not therefore an avoidance tactic, but an essential prerequisite for writing.

Getting started

There nevertheless comes a moment when you must put pen to paper, or, more probably, fingers to keyboard. For most people, this is a profoundly daunting prospect. Faced with the blank page, the empty screen, the unwritten first sentence, all confidence evaporates. How can one possibly commit oneself to any words at all? How does one begin to begin?

There are several answers to this question, or rather tips,

which I have discovered, gleaned and had recommended to me over the years. First, begin at the beginning, but be prepared to discover fairly quickly that it's not the beginning at all. This is the 'Get Anything Down' philosophy, and works on the principle that nothing is more paralysing than searching for that combination of vowels and consonants which will comprise the Perfect First Sentence. School teachers are eager advocates of this approach: 'Write your opening paragraph, then cross it out', they used to tell us over and over again. An advertising copywriter recently told me that he gives the same advice to trainees: 'Write the first page, then throw it away.' In fact, the technique seems to work well for most kinds of writing. That said, some genres will obviously be easier to start than others. The 'once upon a time' formula of the fairy story is an example of probably the easiest. Similarly, one kind of writing may have more hanging on the quality of its opening sentence than another: a company report clearly relies less on its first words than, say, a book review.

Another option is to begin *before* the beginning. This was the advice given me by a friend and fellow author when I was having great difficulty getting started on my second book. The 'Get Anything Down' approach had failed me, the bin was full of discarded first pages, mild hysteria was setting in.

The book in question was based on personal experience of bereavement, and I was finding it very hard to know how much of myself I wanted to reveal, how much of my sorrow and grief I could stand to revisit. I didn't want the book to read like a self-indulgent splurge, nor did I want it to sound too brisk and buttoned-up. How could I speak honestly about the pain of bereavement without making readers feel even worse than they did already? On the other hand, how was I to imbue the text with a sense of hope without seeming to dismiss the anguish of loss?

However hard I tried, I just couldn't seem to strike the right balance. In desperation I rang my friend David. 'I can't do it,' I wailed, 'I can't find the right way to start.' 'How about starting with how you're feeling about starting?' he suggested, 'instead of trying to begin the book, try writing about the difficulties of beginning it. Just sit down and describe your thoughts and feelings.'

I did as he suggested, and found the words pouring on to the page. Two or three thousand words later, I was ready to start writing the book itself. The process of putting into words my unresolved concerns about the book in turn helped me to focus on them and decide what I was going to do about them. It also provided a useful warm-up exercise, a way of getting into the writing without the pressure of producing the real thing.

A third way of breaking the back of that opening sentence is to speak it rather than write it. One author I know always starts in this way. Talking into a tape recorder and then transcribing the words on to paper enables her to overcome the self-consciousness of starting to write. Whether you talk to a tape recorder, a friend, or simply to thin air, describing out loud what it is you are trying to write can help to kick-start the process of writing into action.

Another technique for starting that I have found very useful is to begin by writing in long-hand, rather than directly on to the computer. The hand-written words somehow look less imposing to me than those uniform black shapes on the screen. I feel less awed by them, less in thrall to them, when they are just scruffy squiggles on a sheet of paper. I've heard other people say the opposite: knowing that words on a screen can be deleted at a key-stroke reduces the anxiety of producing them, whereas they feel horribly stuck with words on a page. The trick, I suppose, is to do whatever feels comfortable, to be inventive not only about what you write, but also about how you write it. The main thing is to get started. After all, you can always start again.

Where to write

This summer I began to understand why there's money to be made in out-of-season cottage rentals. Cousins of my husband lent us their home for a fortnight and I experienced for the first time my ideal writing environment: a warm, comfortable, remote house, where the phone never rang, the post was never for me, where there were no responsibilities and no distractions. I wrote three whole chapters in two heavenly weeks.

Writing is seldom this effortless, particularly for women, as this book demonstrates. Perhaps that is why writers are so particular about where and when they write, some insisting they can only write in bed, or in a shed at the bottom of the garden. Natalie Sarraute writes in a cafe; Maya Angelou goes to the extreme of renting a hotel room to work in; Nabokov used to write standing at a lectern in the morning, sitting at a desk in the afternoon, and reclining on a chaise longue in the evening. An enviable few seem able to write anywhere: Isaac Bashevis Singer worked at the kitchen table, and seems to have been wholly unperturbed by interruptions from either phone-calls or visitors.

I tend to be rather a restless writer. I move from room to room. I switch from paper to word-processor and back again. I start writing at a different time each day. I have a routine in order to break it. I also find that different places are good for different stages. In the early phases of a book, I need to feel insulated from the world. This usually means going somewhere I'll be unreachable and undisturbable, but where I'll still feel reasonably at home. This may be the library, or else a cafe in town that I like (it remains something of a mystery to me why household noise should be so intrusive, while the din of a cafe forms a pleasant background hum). Later, when the momentum of the writing is carrying me along, I can work well enough at home at my desk. If I get stuck or have revisions to do, I may again retreat to an anonymous setting away from the house.

When to write

Further to the issue of where to write is the question of when to write. Some people swear by the early morning, before the paraphernalia of the day takes over; others write only at night, presumably for a similar reason. Most writers will have their preferred hours, just as they have their preferred venues. I remember my grandfather shutting himself in his study every morning for two hours in order to write; at the end of that time he would emerge and set off for the office, but as long as he was in there, my grandmother stood Cerberus-like by the door; nothing and nobody was allowed to disturb him. The reality for most writers, however, is that they must seize their moment when it comes: family life and school holidays have no great respect for precious writing routines.

Given the pressure of time and other commitments, as Judith Baxter and Gerrilyn Smith also point out, it's important to know when you are likely to work efficiently and when you're just wasting your energy. For about a year after becoming full-time self-employed I tried to stick to office hours, but however dutifully I sat at my desk, the period after lunch seldom produced anything but lethargy and disaffection. In fact, sitting there with a head full of cotton wool made me downright miserable. Eventually I accepted that while the routine of an office might succeed in obscuring the natural peaks and troughs of concentration, trying to recreate this routine at home was counter-productive. Now, unless I'm up against a totally inflexible deadline, I don't even try to write in the afternoon. Instead I go for a walk, do the shopping, sleep, make phonecalls. By about 3.30 or 4 pm, I'm ready to start again, and can usually put in another two or three hours before stopping for the day.

Most writers have some sort of routine or schedule for their writing. Some set themselves word counts, others block off certain times of the day, others give themselves targets of finishing a certain section by a certain time. George Sand used to set herself a specific number of hours for writing each day. If she reached the end of a piece before the allotted time was up, she would start something new. Trollope, famously, set himself word counts for the day, and would begin a new novel rather than fall short of his target. Graham Greene used the same technique the other way round: he liked to hit his word goal in mid-sentence, so that his unconscious mind had something to be working on over night.

One of my favourite author anecdotes testifies to the fact that it is not always obvious when a writer is writing: in an interview with the Paris Review, the American writer James Thurber confesses, 'I never quite know when I'm not writing. Sometimes my wife comes up to me at a party and says, "Dammit, Thurber, stop writing." She usually catches me in the middle of a paragraph. Or my daughter will look up from the dinner table and ask, "Is he sick?" "No," my wife says, "he's writing something." '

I tend to allot blocks of time rather than word counts, simply because I find some passages come easier than others. I may produce two thousand words one day and no more than two hundred the next, though I sit at my desk for the same amount of time. If things are going well,

I'll go over my allotted time, (nothing is more satisfying than the discovery that several hours have passed like minutes), but if on the other hand things are going badly, I stop. I don't force myself to write when I'm tired, because I usually find afterwards that what I've written is not much good and has to be rewritten anyway. I don't set myself sections to write because I'm hopeless at judging how long any given section will take, invariably under- or over-estimating how straightforward or complicated it will be. I *always* write less than I think I should have done, and am *always* frustrated by how long it seems to take to write anything at all.

Writing is such an individual and idiosyncratic business that it would be impossible – and foolish – to prescribe to anyone else an ideal time or place to work, but a containing framework of some kind seems necessary for the majority of writers, if for no other reason than that writing is a grind as often as it is a pleasure, and incentives help.

Selecting a structure

Non-fiction writing comes burdened with various unhelpful assumptions, none more so than that it benefits from a pre-existing and perfectly logical structure. This allegedly cuts out much of the agony – and the ecstasy – of writing: the author of non-fiction has only to follow the yellow brick road from its start to its finish. Fiction, in contrast, is seen as a profoundly complex and creative process of imaginative journeying. It seems to me, however, that fiction brings with it certain helpful liberties. The fiction writer has the advantage of being able to skip around in a way that the non-fiction writer cannot; fiction allows the writer to play about with locations, perspective, chronology, genres, while non-fiction taxes the writer with its insistent demand for clarity, structure, logic. In addition, non-fiction is supremely intolerant of experimentation and deviation: if the reader can't follow you, you too are lost – not a problem that especially troubled Joyce.

Finding the structure of a piece of non-fiction writing, whether long or short, varies in difficulty according to the subject matter. Some subjects suggest a structure from the outset. My first book was a ghosted autobiography (sadly, it was never published), and the structure in this case was not a problem: I simply followed the actual chronology of the person's life. Similarly, my second book came with a built-in structure: the process of a bereavement, from the early days immediately after the death through the various stages of grief. But my third book, a collection of interviews broadly connected by the theme of working women, suggested two alternative structures: I could either write a text and splice it with extracts from the interviews, or else I could present the interviews intact and then top-and-tail them with text. I opted for the second – and was subsequently criticised by reviewers for having done so! My fourth book, on the role and importance of play in women's lives, suggested no structure whatsoever. Deciding how best to present the material and set forth the argument took almost as much time, and certainly as much effort, as the actual writing. I wanted to find a way of matching structure and content, and found it frustrating that a book on play should be bound by the so unplayful conventions of grammar, layout and debate. French feminist theorists like Monique Wittig have argued persuasively that these conventions are in any case unsuited to women's writing, being fundamentally constructed to serve male ways of thinking and feeling. Since the book was intended to expose how play, like language, has been man-made, and how women's play has, as result, been marginalised and devalued, it seemed particularly inappropriate to adopt these conventional structures. I therefore considered discarding the usual ways of organising an argument; I thought about arranging the words in a zigzag or a circle across the page; I tried abandoning a lone authorial voice and instead creating a symphony of voices. But although I was attracted and excited by the idea of presenting the book in a playful way, ultimately I decided I couldn't take the risk of alienating the reader. I needed to put my ideas across as clearly as possible and, sadly, I decided that meant also conventionally. However enticing, literary antics would have to wait.

Sub-headings, though not always appropriate, can be an invaluable aid through the structural gloom as several other contributors to this book have also pointed out. They give you something to lean on, allow you to survey the view and get your bearings. Judicious sub-headings help the writer to keep the structure tight and on course. Even temporary sub-headings which you may want to remove later provide, like scaffolding, a preliminary form and shape to a piece. Sub-headings also facilitate smooth shifts in pace or tone, for example when changing subject, (equivalent to a novelist's use of a new character or place). Most importantly, sub-headings break the text up into bite-sized chunks, making the writing of it that much more manageable. They serve the same purpose for readers, letting them know where they are and where they're going.

Finding a voice

Akin to selecting a structure is the task of finding a voice. Again, this is taken for granted as one of the essentials of fiction writing, but is often overlooked in nonfiction, where it is just as crucial. Should one be jovial, earnest, confident, diffident? Authoritative, matey, impersonal, friendly? As with the structure, the appropriate voice will be more obvious with some pieces of writing than with others. Choosing the right voice can take a while, and searching for it can be disheartening. It's quite normal, for instance, to hit on just the right tone for Chapter One and find that it's grating horribly by Chapter Four. It is worth bearing in mind, however, that it isn't always necessary to use the same voice throughout; sometimes a piece of writing will require several voices. Also, the right voice may not be one you like, especially having heard it day in day out for months on end. (I often wonder how Jane Austen bore listening to the dreadful Emma Woodhouse during the time it took her to write that novel.) I find it helps to think about the *reader* (surprisingly easy to forget), to ask myself, 'Who am I addressing? How would I speak to her or him if they were in the room with me?' Conversely, I try to forget about what aspect of the *author* I am trying to project: it is easy to become self-conscious when writing, but seldom helpful.

A good editor or agent can be invaluable in guiding you towards the appropriate voice; indeed, their commitment to the project can make them a kind of prototype reader: if they like it, you're on track.

It was not easy finding the right voice for my most recent book, which had to be both scholarly and popular, historical and contemporary, polemical and reasonable, but my editor's enthusiasm for the book gave me the confidence to try and bridge these divides. I regarded her as my ideal reader and trusted her judgement: if she found the tone amenable and convincing, I was content. Then, disaster! With six chapters still to go, she moved to another publishing house! For several weeks I floundered, unable to make any real progress. I had lost my 'reader' and was no longer clear who I was writing for.

Sustaining stamina, maintaining morale

Writing is a physical process as much as a cerebral one. At times it feels like trying to control a runaway coach and twelve. Reining in the various strands of an argument, pulling together all the relevant material, knowing when to go with one train of thought and hold back on another – all this is arduous and tiring. Writing is also, often, dull. There will be moments when the ideas flow and the words fly, when it is all gloriously effortless, and you are dazzled by the accomplishment, originality and importance of your own thoughts. But there are also long stretches when you are bored to death by what you're writing and can't believe anyone else will find it interesting either. Having an idea for a piece of writing is one thing, the process of getting it down on paper is quite another.

It is not at all unusual at some stage in a project to get bogged down, or just plain stuck. This can happen with all kinds of writing, long or short, technical or philosophical. Nearly every writer I've ever known gets about half or three-quarters of the way through a piece of writing and then hits a wall of doubt. 'Is this any good?' you ask yourself. 'Why would anyone want to read this? I haven't anything to say anyway. In fact, I should never have started in the first place.'

Part of the problem is that people have very unrealistic expectations of the experience of writing and are amazed to discover that, like most other work, it involves a large amount of drudgery. The crisis of confidence that so many writers suffer mid-way through a project exposes three of the myths of writing: that it is i) easy, ii) enjoyable, iii) satisfying. It can be all three of these at times; to expect it to be so all of the time is to head for certain disillusionment.

Sometimes getting stuck is an indication that something is wrong, but more often, in my experience at least, it is simply an unavoidable aspect of the writing process. A certain amount of spadework – with the structure, the voice, the concept, the argument – is inevitable, especially with non-fiction, and you just have to battle through the boredom.

Props and tricks

Being somewhat averse to planning, I often find myself romping along for the first few paragraphs, pages or chapters, and then grinding to a soul-destroying halt without a clue where to go next. When this happens I find it helps to fall back on a number of practical techniques, similar to those for getting started on a piece in the first place.

If the problem seems to be to do with the structure or direction of a piece, I will try summarising the work I've done up to that point. On small pieces of paper, I write out short résumés of the existing sections or chapters, and then lay them out in front of me so that I can, quite literally, see where the writing is going. If I've strayed off-course at some stage, it usually becomes apparent where. Seeing the whole piece in précis like this also makes it easier to see where it needs to go next. If for some reason I can't distil the text into short, typed summaries, I try to map the whole work using large sheets of paper and coloured pens. Starting with a keyboard or heading in the centre of the page, I then build up a diagram from that central point of the main themes or points of that section or chapter. Both these techniques provide a visual summary of the text, which can expose the weak links in the chain of an argument or structure, as well as providing an overview of the general shape of a piece, which can help you to see what still needs to be done. More mundanely, they give you something to do other than stare at the screen in those chasmic moments when the brain has stopped functioning and faith in the project has evaporated.

Sometimes the writing dries up, not because of specific problems, but simply because I'm tired or bored. When this happens, I, like Judith Baxter, use various strategies: I try a change of venue, decamping to another room or to the library for the rest of the day, or I use these fallow periods to get on with mechanical tasks which take time but require little imaginative effort, such as the references, bibiliography, page numbering or page layout. If neither of these options help, I'll stop and do something completely different for a while. A walk or swim can be far more effective than sitting slavishly at my desk for two hours.

And finally . . .

If I embark on a writing project with a mixture of enthusiasm and dread, then wade through the middle stages in a soup of doubt and boredom, there will come, I know, that surge of excitement and exhilaration when I at last reach the end. Usually, it comes without warning: just when you're despairing of ever ending, suddenly you're through! You've emerged! You've survived! The best part of writing is not receiving advance copies, or publication day, but the quiet, private moment when you set down that final full stop. It's usually a short-lived moment, for the end of the main text is rarely the end of the job. Quite apart from the nuts and bolts of bibliography, references, notes, acknowledgments and index, there may also be editor's comments to incorporate, page proofs to read, cover blurb and catalogue copy to check. The sensation of finality is as fleeting as it is satisfying, but worth savouring for all that.

Writing isn't a process that stops and starts in a neat, orderly fashion. It comes and goes, ebbs and flows, fits and falters. Like James Thurber, I hardly know when I'm not writing. There is always some project on the go somewhere in my head. At the moment, for example, as I am finishing this chapter, I am also sketching out a book review, revising one of my books for a new edition, preparing the manuscript of another to send to my agent, and gathering material for two new books. Ideas prompt me from bed in the night, just as lack of them may well keep me from my desk the next morning. Writing is a mysterious, compulsive, and at times profoundly rewarding business. I do it because there's nothing else I'd rather do.

As I write this, I am expecting at any moment to give birth to my first child. People say that childbirth and writing are in many ways analogous, but as yet I cannot either agree or disagree. I do know that the two processes share certain similarities, thus far at least: both start small and get bigger and bigger until you wonder how you can possibly sustain and contain them; both tax your patience and endurance; the sheer weight of them wears you out; both make it difficult to sleep at times; both preoccupy you to an extraordinary degree, and both interfere with your ability to concentrate on other people's conversation. Both are also uniquely and preciously the products of your own being. The anxieties and frustrations are yours alone, but so too are the satisfaction and the fulfilment.

I have no idea how parenthood will affect the rhythms and routines of my writing life – drastically, I suspect. The novelist, Candia McWilliam, said in a recent interview that a woman loses two years of writing with every child. I have no doubt that there is a whole separate chapter to be written on the combining of children and writing, but I am not yet qualified to write it. All I know for sure is that while writers may have a great deal in common with one another, writing is ultimately an intensely personal business. To amend Tolstoy's famous phrase, if there are as

many minds as there are heads, then there are as many
ways of writing as there are writers.

Postscript

Shortly after I wrote the above chapter, I went into labour
and, shortly afrter that, became the mother of a little girl.
At the time of correcting the proofs, she has changed from
a tiny infant to an exuberant toddler, and I have acquired
at firsthand some experience of combining children and
writing. I no longer have the luxury of not writing if I'm
tired; not only am I always tired, but with strictly limited
time available for writing each day, I now have to seize the
oportunity however I happen to be feeling. After a year of
broken nights, I was quite proud of my ability to write
reasonably lucid prose through a fog of tiredness.) Before I
had my daughter, I used not to work in the early afternoon; now, I have to work then, for come three o'clock,
my writing time is up and I'm heading off to the childminder.

I have a better appreciation of how crucial good childcare is for a writer who is also a mother, for without our
wonderful, reliable, affordable childminder, Margaret, I
would have found it impossible to continue writing, not
only because it wouldn't have been logistically or financially possible, but because the anxiety I'd feel if I didn't
know for certain that my daughter was being well and
lovingly cared for in my absence would make it extremely
hard to lose myself in my work in the necessary way – a
way that men, I fear, can and do still take for granted.

Having a book and a baby is like having two babies, or
two books, and I feel constantly torn between them,
worried that one gets too much of me and the other is
neglected. Time taken for writing is always too much time

away from my daughter, and time with my daughter means not enough time for my work. And yet I wouldn't want to give up either. With a child in my life, I have become a far more disciplined writer. I get to my desk sooner, and am distracted less easily once there. I can no longer afford to spend time on non-essentials. This means I have become more productive, but it has also increased the slog factor, as I can no longer wait for the perfect moment to come along before I work.

Curiously, none of this has been as disastrous as it may sound. I now achieve more in one hour than I used to in four, and one hour actually now seems longer than four used to. Consequently, I have learnt some of the satisfaction of using time well. I am still writing, despite the difficulties, and that too is a source of satisfaction. The experience of motherhood has sharpened and softened me at the same time, made me more organised, more focused, more rigorous, but also more responsive, more empathetic, more reflexive. All of this feeds back into my work, into my writing, and while I don't pretend to like feeling tired, or having no discernible short-term memory, or having to read some sentences several times before their meaning goes in, I am by no means ready to close up my lap top. Quite the opposite: there is more than ever to write about and, more than ever, reason to write it.

Twelve 'rules'
Sue Roe

Previous pages have revealed some of the similarities and
differences within women's writing practices. Here are the
twelve 'rules' that work best for me:

1. Love your subject. You will probably have to live with
   it for a long time. Expect to immerse yourself in the
   world of whatever it is you are researching. If you are
   writing biography or criticism, you are likely to begin
   by empathising with your subject; after a while you
   may start to feel as if you *are* that person. You will enter
   the world you are researching wholly, wholeheartedly.
   You will become obsessed by every detail of it. You
   will become determined to leave no stone unturned,
   and you will develop a missionary zeal about converting your reader. If you are going to sustain that kind of
   energy, and let it into your writing, you should only be
   persuaded to write about something you love in the
   first place. There will be stages in the process that will
   convince you you are in purgatory, so make sure they
   are stages you know you will pass through. If you love
   your subject you will communicate your attachment,
   your fascination, and your writing will feel alive.

2. Split it into sections. Make categories. The material
   required to write a book is substantial. It will

overwhelm you unless you compartmentalise it from the start. Embark on one bit of the project at a time. Most items of information will – maddeningly – fit into several or even all of your categories. Be ruthless as you research. Allocate your material to one section or aspect of the book or another. If later you want to re-structure and/or re-arrange, you will do so with conviction rather than with a feeling of indecision and muddle. Keep the project tidy – whether you do so in documents on your computer or in a pile of cardboard files. If you know where you have put a thing, you will know where to find it when you come to look for it. At first, you may imagine you will be able to store everything in your head. You won't.

3. Keep your audience in mind. Always remember, from the outset, who you are writing for. It's a good idea to consult your publisher about this. Publishers know their own markets and if your book is commissioned it will have been commissioned for a purpose. Who will buy it when it's finished? Why? What will they really need to know? If you love your subject you will enjoy the added advantage of the knowledge that you are writing it for yourself, but yourself is not your first priority. Your responsibility is to your reader. Don't take too much for granted, and don't patronise. Address your reader in a reasonably consistent tone. Determine the sort of reader your book is for (even have an imaginary – or a real – reader in mind) and write for her/him. Invent a quite discriminating reader, one with a sense of humour if possible. Keep in mind her or his level of discernment, her or his needs.

4. Follow your hunches. Don't abandon a lead until you are sure it really will yield nothing. By the time

you come to narrow your research down to specifics, to hunt down particular items of information, you should have read widely in your field and have developed a feel for your project. Sometimes tangential insights can offer you a new take on your overall plan. Incidental detail, the odd quirky item, is interesting, and may be amusing. Offer a new angle. Hold your reader's attention. It's what you *didn't* know before, and couldn't possibly have discovered for yourself, that entices you, as a reader. At the same time, don't just be eccentric. Cover the ground. Let your reader trust you, then you'll be trusted with the quirks, the spice.

5. Expect it to expand. Don't get exasperated as you discover that your project has begun to sprawl alarmingly. It has burst the banks of the archive you thought entirely contained it. There are bits of information you need to track down in Scarborough, Toulouse, Cardiff. Track them down. Regard it as a treasure hunt. If all the information you need were stored tidily in a predictable bibliography located conveniently in one place, there would be no need for your book. If you are writing about a potholer, go potholing. If your subject spent a week in Cromer, go to Cromer. Read all the letters she or he wrote in Cromer. Compare her/his Cromer with yours. What is the best possible location to steep yourself in the atmosphere of the next bit of your project? Go there. Do it. Experience it. Understand it from the inside, as well as from the outside. Then come back and apply the force of that other hat: your organising hat. Discover it, do it, make a note of it, file it.

6. Consult the experts. Know what you are capable of learning on the job, and what others have already put

well in order. It is tempting to begin to think you can, or must, re-invent the wheel in this book of yours. Remember, you can't be an expert in every single aspect of it. If there is work you need to incorporate that others have already dealt with, discoveries which need to be acknowledged, which have already been made, go to the most reliable source you can find. Do not forget to acknowledge. Or to thank.

7. Find the centre of gravity. Heinrich Von Kleist, in his enchanting essay 'On the Marionette Theatre', describes asking a puppet operator how to pull the strings so that each of the puppet's separate limbs moves in the rhythm of the dance. The answer, of course, is that you do not move each separate limb, you find the puppet's centre of gravity. Once you have done this, the limbs move themselves, and the puppet 'actually' *is* dancing. It is part-concentration, part-magic. The same applies to music, drawing, and to writing. How to find the appropriate voice to address your reader in? This is your creative struggle, and it draws on your imagination, your flair, your sense of style, and again, on your perception of the character of your reader. Do not instruct. Evoke, attract, enlighten, enhance. Nobody wants to be ordered around by an author, everybody likes the opportunity to envisage, identify, imagine. Be playful, be seductive, make your book an enchanting, challenging place to be.

8. Translate, transpose, transform. Do not blind your reader with science. Talk onto the page. If you can't imagine *saying* it, in a conversation or within a group of people, don't write it. Never, never use language to obscure. Speak the language of your reader. Books are for communicating.

9. Be deferential. You are necessarily entering a world in which others will have worked for years. Respect their views, even if yours are different. Books which display a friendly approach to the work of others are more appealing than those which seem to exist entirely in isolation. The business of referring to and acknowledging the work of others is difficult. It's tricky, it's tiring, but your reader is more likely to want to enter a wide, garrulous world than a restricting, enclosed one.

10. Expect to have to write this thing over and over again. Draft and re-draft. Practise, practise, practise. You would not expect to be able to perform a piece of music without practising it. What looks spontaneous is usually arrived at gradually. Draft bits of the book as you research it, then expect to have to re-draft the whole thing again once you have put it all together. The business of communicating directly, without clutter, in a conversational tone is only arrived at once your material is completely ordered and absolutely within your control. When you arrange your deadline, remember to take account of this.

11. Take breaks from it, in the final stages. As you complete bits, keep sending them away. Get piles of hard copy off your desk. Put them in box files, put them in drawers, give them to people to read, or just to hide for you. While a piece of writing is still in the room, still in the house, it will feel unfinished. Send it away, as a test. If you feel relieved when it has gone, you have probably finished it. If it continues to nag at you, niggle at you, disturb your dreams, then maybe that bit you thought you ought to put in but at the last minute decided not to, should be included after all. Try not to spend too many hours staring into

space with it spread all over your lap. Somehow things begin to disintegrate from within if you do that. Send them away, read them when they come back, and your judgement will be clearer.

12. Meet your deadline. This is the best way to pace yourself, retain your sanity, and maintain your reputation with your publisher. Things tend to have a shelf life in your head. If you need a margin for errors, it's best built in at the beginning of your schedule, rather than at the end. There is another good reason why you should meet your publisher's deadline. Publishers commission books into a world they can predict and foresee, partly because to some extent they are creating it. They make specific plans for their lists, having in mind the predictable needs of their markets, and the environment they are creating by commissioning the range of books in their lists. If you deliver your book late you may not be pitching it into the environment your publisher has envisaged being able to sell it in. Once the project is past its sell-by date, it may be more difficult to launch it. But remember also that sell-by date in your own head. You can only maintain the degree of energy you need, the momentum to sustain this particular project, for so long. After that, you will keep going, but not with the same dynamic. Well, we are all of us sometimes a *bit* late, and of course there are such things as unforeseen circumstances. But if you have a goal, you are more likely to meet it. Rule thirteen would be: don't be too hard on yourself if you don't. Tomorrow is another day.

PUBLISHERS AND AGENTS

Contacting a publisher
Gill Davies

There are two sorts of author who do not need help with contacting a publisher. The first are authors who have an established record of successful books behind them. They will be given a warm welcome. The second are authors who have managed to persuade a literary agent to work on their behalf. In this case, the agent does all the spadework involved in approaching suitable publishers, talking through the publishing proposal and hammering out the contract. Alas, there are relatively few enlightened agents who are still prepared to take on untried authors. If you are such an author, and think you may need a literary agent, some of the advice offered in this chapter could equally well be used when persuading an agent to act on your behalf. (See also Dorothy Lumley's chapter.)

Any working editor can testify to the fact that there are thousands of authors beavering away at their books who appear not to have the slightest idea about who the 'right' publisher for their books would be. Or indeed how to go about contacting a publisher. As Frances Arnold has pointed out, more publishing projects get turned down on the grounds that, 'Alas, your book would not be suited for our list', than any other I can think of. It is true that this much-resorted-to rejection often masks the real truth, that the editor thinks the material is abysmal but is trying to be kind. There are, however, authors who genuinely have decent books that deserve to be published but do not seem to know how to go about achieving that.

Many of them will have scrutinised reference books on publishing, such as *Writers' and Artists' Yearbook* or the *Cassell's Directory of Publishing*. Excellent books though they are, they inevitably have drawbacks. When a publisher lists subjects published – history or biography for example – there are no clues as to the type of book in those subjects. Furthermore, the lists reflect the range of books in print with the publisher; not necessarily what the publisher is looking for at the moment.

Often just plain commonsense is what a new author – or the author moving into a new field – needs when embarking on the long haul getting a book published. And stamina, and a thick skin, because the whole process can be drawn out and can certainly test the author's sensitivity. This is probably no bad thing, since, as many published authors will testify, writing a book is not suitable activity for the faint-hearted.

Selecting a publisher

As Frances Arnold has shown, there is absolutely no point in sending a travel book to a publisher who specialises in gardening books, or non-fiction to a fiction publisher, or an academic book to a general publisher. Researching the publisher is crucial.

The second principle is to select a publisher. This is more complicated than checking to see whether they publish in your area or not – they are likely also to be catering for particular types of reader. Those calling themselves, for example, history publishers, will tend to specialise in one of a variety of 'histories': popular, textbook, scholarly, educational. The greatest divide in publishing is between general (or consumer) books and specialist ones.

General books are aimed at the 'ordinary reader', requiring no particular knowledge in order to be read and enjoyed. Specialist books are aimed at readers with, as is implied, specialist knowledge or experience. Typically such books are academic, educational, professional and scientific books, or books for enthusiasts who have developed in-depth knowledge in their subject. General and specialist publishing require quite different sales, marketing and promotion treatment, and prospective authors should take care in judging which category their book falls into.

It is important that the prospective author grasps the essential connection between subject matter and type of readership because the combination of the two is the key to the identity of the publishing house and, it follows from that, determines the kind of book a house is looking for.

Newspaper and magazine reviews can give hints about publishers' lists, and it is worth noting the publishers of books that bear some relation to the one you are writing. However, only a very small selection of the books that get published every year actually receive a review and they are books written either by popular or prestigious authors, or reflect the tastes or interests of the reviews editor, or have been pushed hard by the publicity managers in our publishing houses.

It is therefore usually more profitable to visit a good bookshop. The range of titles stocked in the shops of the national chains and in some of our excellent local bookshops is, still, remarkable. Several visits to different shops, and a few hours study of the appropriate shelves, should tell you who is currently publishing what, and the kind of readership they are trying to reach. You can carry out the same kind of exercise in a library, but, sadly, since library funds are rapidly diminishing these days, a broad range of new books is often simply not there to be found.

There are other sources you can turn to. For example,

if you are an academic, the chances are that you have colleagues in the department of the institution where you teach or do research who have had books published. Once someone has been published they become much more knowledgeable about publishing in general and their publishers in particular. What's more, academics tend to talk about their books and their publishers, and compare notes. These days there is a lot of pressure within the university sector for researchers and lecturers to publish, and as a result there is a continuous, informal network of information in full swing, with individuals passing 'intelligence' to each other about which publishing houses are looking for what material at the moment, what the editors in the house are like, whether the publisher's marketing is up to scratch, and so on.

Generally speaking, a published author (whatever the genre of writing) is a very useful source of information. Not only have they become knowledgeable about publishing, but they have become sensitised to what is good, bad and indifferent in publishing. They have been there before you and have experience they can pass on. If you do not work in an environment such as academia where writing and books are an implicit part, or if you do not have a published author you can get in contact with, then it is a good idea to seize the moment if you do meet a published writer. You might come across one teaching a seminar or workshop you attend, or perhaps at a writing class, or at a bookshop reading where the public is invited to meet the author. Of course, the author might have other things on her or his mind at that moment and discretion should always be used, but if you find yourself within arms' length of that author, it is worth trying to ask some questions. Never ask them if they would read your material and give you advice. It is highly unlikely that they have either the time or the inclination to provide this service.

Finally, do, as Frances Arnold suggests, get hold of publishers' catalogues and read them carefully. These days bookshops tend not to keep catalogues in any quantity because the shops are bursting with stocks of books and there is precious little room for anything else, so the way to do it is to ring the publishers and ask to be sent the catalogues you are interested in. Be fairly precise about this. If you are writing a history book, or if cookery or travel is your subject, ask for the appropriate catalogues. If the person at the end of the telephone asks if you want to see a catalogue for new books or backlist (that is, books that have been in print for a year or more), ask to see both because only that way will you get to examine both the breadth and the depth of publications which the publisher handles.

Catalogues should be read with care because they can be revealing. The title listings and descriptions should confirm whether or not the publisher is going to be interested in principle in the subject of your book. The way in which the descriptions are presented should also reveal whether they are trying to serve the kind of reader you have in mind for your book. Pricing is also instructive. High prices reflect the publishers' view that they are serving the 'top end of the market': books either for the well-heeled and highly educated who have spending power; or books for the committed, that is, the reader who is a serious enthusiast for the subject or needs to buy books that will help them with their studies or their work, and is prepared to pay that little bit more because they will use the book over and over again. Low prices reflect the publisher's aim to reach the 'ordinary reader' who might read the book and then discard it.

There are two other guidelines to use, which are

inter-related: the number of titles listed and the dates of publication. First, how many books in a subject has the publisher produced? If there are only a handful of books then you could ask yourself if the publisher had a flirtation with the subject but lost interest, perhaps because the books were not very successful. Look at the year of publication. If these books were published several years ago, then you might well be suspicious that the publisher did indeed 'have a go' but is not committed to the subject now. On the other hand, if those comparatively few titles were published in the last couple of years, you may be witnessing a publisher's entry into a particular market and subject and that they will be looking to add more books. Substantial numbers of titles, and currency in their publication, is good, hard evidence that the publisher is committed to that field and will be on the look out for more. A catalogue that reveals books that are ageing suggests either that the publisher or in-house editor has lost interest in the subject, or even that the house does not currently have an editor with the experience or 'feel' for the field. Editors do move on from one publishing house to another and sometimes when they leave, they cannot easily be replaced.

If at the end of these various exercises you conclude that you still can't find the right publisher then either you have written the most extraordinarily unusual book (rare, but it does occasionally happen), or you are fooling yourself that your book is unique. Of course your book is unique because only you have written it, but in fact most books fall into one of many types and by using the combination of subject and market (readership), you should be able to classify your book and identify the kind of publisher who might be interested in it.

Contacting a publisher

We could say 'Publishers' here. These days it is permissible to approach more than one publisher at the same time. In the past, an editor would dispatch authors' manuscripts or proposals back to them with a note of disapproval at the first whiff of another publisher being on the scene. It is now accepted that getting published is a difficult and competitive business and that authors do need to shop around. However, if you do submit your proposal or manuscript to several houses, beware of conspicously play-ing the field, of playing one editor off against another. Most editors (especially the experienced), have been in that situation before and will not be subjected to that kind of pressure. Only authors with some success behind them have the power to play that game.

Having selected your publishers, it is worth ringing them to get the name of the editor or editorial director who handles the relevant list, so that you know precisely to whom your letter and material should be addressed. Also, editors, for perfectly human reasons, appreciate being identified. 'Dear Gill Davies' always goes down better than 'Dear Sir or Madam'. Someone has gone to the bother of finding out.

If you want to make sure of the form in which the editor likes to receive material (proposal or manuscript), ask to speak to him or her. The chances are that you will not speak directly to the editors but to their assistants. The assistants should be able to specify whether a proposal or manuscript is preferable at this stage and should also be able to outline how a proposal should be presented. (See also Frances Arnold's and Gerrilyn Smith's chapters.)

Whoever you speak to at the publishers, keep it brief. You are simply asking for advice on how to proceed. Editorial staff will give pointers, probably by telling you that you should outline the market for the book, give thorough chapter descriptions, state the length of the book, and its completion date, at the very least, but they don't have the time to talk at length to everyone who calls.

First-time authors frequently ask if they can come into the house to meet the editor for a 'little chat' about the book before submitting the material. Alas, the editor is unlikely to agree to that unless the prospective author is, for example, a journalist whose work the editor knows and therefore has some grasp of both the journalist's written style and ability to marshall ideas and information. Editors receive, quite commonly, hundreds of submissions every year, the majority of which will not see the light of day. They cannot see all prospective authors and don't like to make exceptions in some cases and not others, without good reason.

The proof of the pudding is in the eating. You will be judged by the proposal or manuscript you submit. Can you marshall your arguments or information; is the quality of your writing convincing and attractive; do you understand the needs of your readers? At this stage, your ability as a writer is what is most important.

By and large, in non-fiction publishing, as Frances Arnold points out, it is wiser to submit a proposal before embarking on the work of writing a whole manuscript. A proposal gives both you and the editor the chance to test the idea, work on the idea, improve the content and structure of the book, and generally plan ahead for its publication. It is better to start to build the book from the ground up, with the editor's complete involvement and with other expertise which the editor can bring into play, whether it is through advisers, or marketing or production colleagues. All these people can play a large part in helping make your book a better and more successful one.

However, it would be thoroughly wrong to suggest that

authors who have a complete manuscript to hand have been wasting their time. There is an undoubted advantage to a complete script, in that the editor can readily see exactly what your book is, with all its strengths and weaknesses. You should prepare yourself, however, for inevitable revisions.

Writing a proposal

As a number of authors in this book have pointed out, writing a proposal is a good exercise in itself, because it forces you to sit down and think through the book in a detailed way. It requires that you construct the book before you write it.

A proposal should have, at the very least, the following component parts:

1. *A rationale for the book.* Why is it needed, or wanted? What gap is it filling, or why does it supercede what is already in print? What knowledge do you have of the subject and the market that has led you to conclude that this book will find a ready readership? What is your qualification for writing this book? (See also Frances Arnold's chapter.)

2. *A description (two or three paragraphs) of what will go in every chapter.* Spell out what will appear in every chapter – a list of topics or issues to be covered is not sufficient. You must link them so that the editor (and the editor's adviser) can follow your thinking. This is particularly important when the book you are proposing is likely to be controversial or will require a fair amount of theoretical discussion. You will need to demonstrate that you will be able to provide detailed evidence of all your claims and arguments.

3. *An analysis of the likely readership for the book.* It is

important that you exercise some discipline here. As Frances Arnold has shown, many authors are prone to list readerships for their books that are wildly optimistic. Academics, for example, will list academic book buyers but often go on to claim 'the intelligent lay reader' as a probable buyer. The latter will seldom buy academic books that are written in academic language, using highly specialist theory, even if the topic is of current widespread interest. They do not like and are not comfortable with academic writing; they like to read material that comes in a more easily digestible form. So, when defining your readership, stick to readers you are absolutely confident will want the book you are writing and in the form in which it is presented. It is far better to keep your readership definition focused but sound.

4. *An accurate assessment of both the length of the book and the delivery date.* First, length is important because the editor will need to gauge whether you can cover the ground in the number of words you are proposing (especially if your book looks on the short side), or whether you are intending to write a blockbuster – a book that will be very long and therefore expensive to produce, and eventually give the editor pricing problems (see also Frances Arnold's chapter). Editors are often asked 'What is the ideal length for a book?'. The answer is that there is no such thing. However, as a rough, very rough, rule of thumb, anything under 50,000 words is on the short side, anything over 100,000 is getting a bit big for comfort, unless you are writing an absolutely exhaustive, definitive piece and there is a guaranteed, very substantial readership for it.

Delivery is important to the editor because she or he can then plan ahead for the book's appearance in future programmes. The delivery date you offer will appear in your contract, and it becomes a legal obligation on you. If you are late, the editor is within her or his rights to cancel your contract, and will cancel it if you have chosen to write a book that is of current interest now but might be out of fashion if the book appears late (see also Lynette Owen's chapter on publishing contracts). Even if topicality is not an issue, editors do not like authors who deliver late, although it must be said that 'slippage' as it is called, is very common. It is far better to offer up your most pessimistic assessment for delivery and keep to it, than to be optimistic and fail. Writing books takes far longer than most people realise, so thinking this through carefully is important.

5. *An analysis of books either in print or in preparation which could compete with yours.* Since you know your subject well, you may be more familiar than the editor is with what has been written and what those books are like. Present a 'Strengths and Weaknesses' analysis of those other books and clearly demonstrate to the editor why yours will be superior. Saying 'they aren't very good; mine is better' is common in proposals, but rarely impresses editors. If you believe that yours is the very first book on the subject, check this out carefully; if the editor knows of others, your proposal is likely to be returned, and if you do make this claim, you are likely to have to stand by it.

Having written your proposal or put your manuscript into good shape, send it off, with a brief covering letter. The letter should pull out the main points you want to leap out at the editor: what the book is about, what market need it meets, and why you are qualified to write it. It shouldn't need saying, but it does, that your covering letter should be well written, without grammatical, spelling and other errors. Nor should it be written on lined notepaper in green ink. A surprising number of these do reach our desks.

The process leading to a publishing decision

Having sent your material off to a publisher, or publishers, you are likely to need both patience and a strong nerve. In the mind's eye of most prospective authors is an editor who opens up your letter or package, reads it straightaway and then rings or writes you a letter. Anxiety can mount as silence ensues, perhaps broken only by a formal and impersonal note that acknowledges receipt of your material. Unfortunately, back in the publishers' offices, editors are literally fighting for time to read material that comes in. Editors will already have a sizeable pile of material waiting to be read. Yours must join the queue.

The chances are that you might wait two months or more before you get a response containing any real substance. Editors are handling very many books in the course of a year and they are really pushed to read the material that is presented to them. Often, editors are trapped in their own success. The more good books they publish, the more authors want to publish with them.

Unless you are exceptionally lucky, you are not likely to hear anything from the editor for, at the very least, a month and you ought to make plans to take your mind off what is happening to your material. There are hopeful authors who think it is perfectly appropriate to start chasing the editor after a week! Usually this takes the form of phone calls asking 'What is happening?'. The honest answer is 'Nothing. Your proposal is in the middle of pile three and I will get around to it as soon as I can.' Most editors really do not mind explaining how slow the process can be to authors who have no idea about how much material comes into a house every day; and most authors, once they have formed a truer picture of the pressure on editors, will accept that it will take time, but that the editor will eventually be reading their material.

Far more trying are authors (mostly men I have to say) who approach editors imperiously: 'Are you reading it? When are you going to read it? Are you going to publish it? I think you'll find it is publishable and I'll want to hear from you very quickly', and so on. Unfortunately, these authors have misread the situation. They will have demo-cratically to wait in line until their material is at the top of the pile, when it will be judged solely on its merit.

Once editors have read the material, there are various questions they need to answer for themselves.

1 Is this a subject that we publish or want to publish?
2 Do we know, on the basis of the sales of past, similar books, that there is a market for the book?
3 How is the author going to treat the subject? Is it different or an improvement on what has been pub-lished before?
4 Does the author appear to have writing ability?
5 Is the quality of the content, at the very least, acceptable?

If the editor is looking for a book that is going to break new ground, then the answers to questions 1 and 2 may have to be satisfied by some additional market research on the part of the editor (in which you might play your part by supplying additional material). However, most of the time editors are working on subjects and in markets that they know, understand and have experience in. To a degree, editors are working retrospectively; they are look-ing over their shoulders and replicating publishing they know works.

If the editor is able to answer 'yes' to questions 1 and 2,

then they can move swiftly to 3, 4 and 5 because these concern content and how the author presents material. As regards question 3, the editor is looking for a treatment of a subject that is either original or different or replicates a well-established formula that works. Examples of the latter would be classes of romantic fiction, good 'hands-on' cookery and gardening books, textbooks. We know from many years experience that there is a strong, on-going demand for this kind of material. Examples of the former are, well, very hard indeed to define and it would be a fool's errand to try to attempt it.

In fact, original publishing is very rare and despite all the well-known stories about brilliant books that were turned down by publishers, which the rejected author will remind the editor of, the fact is that experienced editors do recognise a good book when they see it. Publishers tend to get remembered for the books they got wrong rather than the ones they got right. The truth about publishing is that every day in publishing offices editors are mostly spending their time judging whether the treatment of a subject is more than adequate in terms of comprehensiveness, focus, logic, accuracy, user-friendliness; whether it competes with other titles in print; whether it is too long or too short; if it will be expensive to produce and to market; rather than chewing on a pencil and wondering if this is an original masterpiece or not.

We now turn to writing ability. If someone can write, it is immediately apparent to the person reading his or her book. One becomes engaged with the writing, one can follow it, one is persuaded, one wants to read on. However, with specialist books in particular, a facility to write does not always go hand in glove with a thorough grasp of the subject. Editors become quite familiar with the subjects they publish but in order to make absolutely sure that they have judged the quality of the material correctly, they tend to use outsider 'readers' or advisers, as several chapters have mentioned. The readers are people who are expert in their fields and can comment in detail on a proposal or manuscript. An editor will be highly influenced by what this adviser has to say and will reject a book if the adviser counsels against it. If the adviser gives an absolute or modified signal of approval, however, you are probably well on your way to a contract. If the adviser asks for modifications to your manuscript or proposal, it is then the task of the editor and author together to work out what is acceptable and desirable for both sides. The editor will not be sympathetic to authors who declare that they cannot change a word and the author should remember that the adviser's reaction is the first indicator of how the outside world might receive the book. Using an adviser is therefore an important aspect of quality control.

Advisers' reports can range from the downright condemnatory to the ecstatically approving. Such extremes are rare in practice. Usually the adviser will turn a book down through a systematic process of pointing out weaknesses in argument, presentation and inaccurate claims for readership. If the adviser is inclined to recommend publication it is quite common, nevertheless, for the adviser to suggest a reordering of the structure, that a chapter be dropped, or added, if he or she feels it is necessary to strengthen the book. By and large advisers see their function as trying to be helpful to both publisher and author.

Through the advisory process, and especially if it is a synopsis which is under scrutiny, the adviser might call in questions about writing ability. If there is any doubt about the fluency or persuasiveness of the synopsis, then the adviser will recommend that the editor see one or two sample chapters. It is not in your interest to refuse to provide them, although authors are known to say that they do not want to go to the trouble of writing chapters without a contract first. The editor's inevitable reply is going to be that only the sample material will clinch matters, perhaps privately remarking to him or herself, 'Well, do you want to write the book or don't you?'. Resistance to supplying sample material is bound to undermine the editor's confidence in your commitment and certainly is not a tactic to be used in forcing a contract if there is any uncertainty about the book.

So, what else is the editor thinking about? Some more questions:

Should this book be in hardback or paperback, or be published simultaneously in both formats?

The answer to this question will be defined in terms of market potential. If there is evidence of substantial, ongoing library sales for the kind of material on offer, then the book is likely to be published in hardback first, with a paperback for individual purchases coming later. Here the publisher is getting two bites of the sales cherry in order to maximise revenue. If not, the book will probably be published in paperback straightaway. Specialist academic or professional publishers will probably hedge their bets by producing a small number of hardbacks for, usually, institutional libraries and academic sales around the world while reserving their greatest firing power for the sales of paperbacks to individuals – hence the simultaneous formats.

In the past, publishers were either hardback or paperback publishers but now most produce a mixture of both. Publishers have a quite distinct view of these formats. For example, some publishers will publish hardbacks only for libraries and for academic and professional sales because they perceive this to be the format these markets want.

The publishers are producing books that will be read over and over again and require the strength of a hardback binding. Other publishers will concentrate on paperback only because they are serving the needs of individual purchasers who want to buy their books in the cheaper format. Clearly much depends on the publisher's position which is determined by the subject matter the house publishes and the profile of the market for that subject.

How many copies would be printed?

Quite simply what the computer suggests I should. All publishers have computer-generated sales records which they can refer to. The editor is likely to look up the sales of books published which are in one way or another similar to the book under consideration and use that number for guidance. In order to control costs, the editor is likely to print the minimum quantity that makes economic sense (the number of copies printed determines the unit cost of each book – ie the more you print the less each book individually costs – and this determines prices). Today, printing technology allows us to reprint very rapidly, and enables us to print smaller quantities without books going out of stock.

Will this book have export potential?

For specialist books there is often an international market of enthusiasts who want to buy the latest thing in their subject and can read English. This is particularly so for academic and professional books. It stands to reason, however, that a book on British gardening or cookery is not going to be relevant to the needs of overseas readers. However, a travel book could sell well overseas in places where British tourists go. Here again, the publishing house's computer is going to be useful because sales can be broken down into home and export sales and can be scrutinised.

British publishers are very export-oriented for historical and cultural reasons. The most important export territory for many books is North America and British publishers treat North America in one of two ways. Either they have a tie up with a distributor and all their books get marketed there (commonly the procedure for specialist publishers in academic, scientific and professional publishing), or they sell North American rights in specific titles to publishers in that territory when they think there is genuine potential for sales (usually the case for general publishers). Sometimes the two are combined: the publisher distributes only those titles where rights have not been sold.

There will be other questions that the editor will be mulling over, concerning the production costs of the book, and whether the house has all the marketing resources to ensure the book can be sold to its maximum potential. Eventually, all these strands come together in a projected profit-and-loss account for each individual book. This will show the anticipated sales revenue from which is subtracted costs (production, ie paper, printing, typesetting, freelance editing costs, illustrator's fees, royalties and marketing expenses) to give a profit figure. These days most houses have a desired target figure (which must include a contribution to the publishers' overheads: heating and lighting, staff salaries, office equipment and so on) which editors must demonstrate they can meet. If they can meet it for your book, and if all other requirements in terms of length of the book, delivery date, and content can be met by you, a contract will be on its way provided the editor can jump one final hurdle.

Most houses have publishing committees which meet on a regular basis to decide which candidates for publication should go forward to contract. In some houses (usually general publishers) marketing and sales executives have great power and can override an editor's recommendation that a contract be offered. In specialist houses, the editor's persuasive arguments are likely to be taken much more seriously because colleagues know that the book will succeed on content. In general publishing, sometimes, a bad book can succeed simply because an energetic sales and marketing department knows just how to promote it in order to catch the public's eye. But, conversely, a good or worthy book can be overruled by marketing because they can't get an 'angle' on it. Whatever the power relations within a house, the author is dependent on the editor to be absolutely convincing when presenting her or his book for publication. A strong publishing proposal is the best way to get an editor galvanised. Nevertheless, an author and editor can go through a great deal of work together, only to be bitterly disappointed when the publications committee turns it down. It does happen.

In all this you might ask, will I get to meet my editor? If you live abroad or a long way from your publisher then you might not. Otherwise, in all probability, you will. It is almost inevitable that during the course of getting the detail of the book right, the editor will want to meet you. This kind of work can be done more quickly and effectively face-to-face rather than through a long exchange of letters. And, after all, the relationship between an editor and an author is a close one which may develop over several years. The editor understands the advantages that come from knowing an author and being able to work in a friendly but professional fashion with her or him. Remember that the relationship between your editor and you is one of mutual self-interest. Your editor wants and needs your book to succeed as much as you do. That is a pretty good basis on which to meet.

I began this chapter by reference to the abundance of hopeful authors who seem to have no grasp of how to go about choosing the right publishers or contacting them. I suspect there are several factors operating in the background. The first is that readers and authors may not be as 'publisher conscious' as those of us who work in the industry believe. We like to think that our publishing houses are synonymous with certain sorts of publishing. The fact is that there are very few houses that have a brand identity so strong that everyone knows (or think they know) exactly what those houses publish. Second, publishing houses do change their identity over time, and in recent years that change has been far more rapid and sustained. It is not that easy for those outside publishing to catch up with that change. Third, many authors put all their efforts, understandably enough, into their writing without realising that a separate, preliminary, effort has to be put into the choice of publisher and making contact with the house. It simply is not wise to proceed at random because publishers do have distinct identities and positions in the marketplace which determine everything they do. Authors need, for their own sakes, to do some market research at this stage and to plan accordingly. Not only will it save you possible disappointment and wasted time, but also publishers are inevitably impressed by authors who have used real judgement in their choice of publisher and made the effort to put their approach and material together in a way that helps the editor in the process of decision making.

It helps if you're famous: A literary agent's view
Dorothy Lumley

Look at any bestseller list and you'll see that many of the top-selling non-fiction books at any one time have media or 'personality' connections. Tie-in TV series on cookery or gardening. World leaders' autobiographies. Inspiring life stories by people who have survived terrible events or illness against all odds. True crime. Stories about soap opera stars, sports personalities . . .

If you're famous, fine. If not, don't despair. Many successes are not the overnight events they appear to be. Delia Smith wrote cookery books for ten years before her first TV series in the early 1980s set her on her way to superstardom. The incredibly successful gardening books by Dr Hessayon have sold in huge quantities on their own merit without much extra media 'hype'. Word-of-mouth recommendation from friend to friend can and does work in establishing new writers.

Does having a literary agent help writers get established or accelerate their success? What exactly does an agent do? Here are some of the pros and cons.

What can an agent do for you?

The Society of Authors carried out a survey among its members a few years ago, to find out whether those members with agents were more likely to get publishing contracts than those without, and whether the terms of those deals were better than for non-agented writers. The results seemed to indicate that having an agent didn't make a crucially significant difference to getting published. Contractual terms, however, did tend to be slightly better if negotiated by an agent.

Patience, perseverance, persistence on the part of a writer do pay off. I firmly believe that 'quality will out'. If you have something worthwhile, it will sell to a publisher in the end, as long as you don't give up.

However, it could well be that a literary agent might speed up the process of selling your work. The agent's job is to meet and talk with editors and publishers to find out what they are looking for, and to develop relationships so that those editors will know that material from that agent is worth paying attention to. So an agent should, in theory, be able to target material more accurately, and have inside information about new lists being started up, old ones folding, editors moving on and so on.

Agents also chase editors for decisions on manuscripts or proposals, for contracts, money owing, cover proofs due, copies of the finished book, information about sales and publicity, royalties and so on. This can save the author a great deal of time, but, perhaps more importantly, the agent may have more 'bargaining power' than the individual author and get responses from publishers more quickly.

Perhaps the most crucial function of the literary agent for many writers is the support they provide in what can be a very lonely profession. The agent can give encouragement during the lean years of rejection slips, and a rudder during sometimes stormy relationships with publishing companies.

In recent years, the publishing business has become very

unsettled. Editors change jobs regularly, many are made redundant. In these cases, the agent becomes the stable contact in the writer's life, providing a fixed point of security while all else changes at bewildering speed.

Many agents have previously been editors, or have worked in other publishing fields, and therefore understand more or less how it all works. They can explain the vagaries of different publishers' procedures and smooth the way for the writer and her or his book.

Choosing an agent

The lists of agents in the *Writers' and Artists' Year Book* and *The Writer's Handbook* are very comprehensive. Each entry covers the kinds of material the agent specialises in. Non-fiction authors should concentrate on those agents who go into more detail about their non-fiction than fiction. A few handle non-fiction only.

Some agencies are one-person outfits, and some are big conglomerates which have a large number of agents operating under one umbrella. The latter usually have different departments dealing with serial rights, translation rights, American rights, and so on. You need to ask yourself which type of operation would suit you better. Do you want an agent with more departments or do you want a lot of editorial input and regular contact? If an agent offers to take you on, it would be as well to discuss the ways in which they work, and see if these suit your tastes.

If you don't have contacts in the world of publishing and agents, a good way to gather information might be to join a writers' group. (Local libraries are most likely to have advertisements.) Writers' groups vary wildly, so feel free to shop around. There are also writing magazines, such as *Writers' Monthly, Freelance Writing and Photography*, and advice books for writers (see bibliography). And there

---

---

are various professional societies, such as the Society of Authors, the Writers' Guild, and many more (see the list in the *Writers' and Artist' Yearbook*), though you usually need to have been published at least once to join. There are networks of seminars, writing weekends, conferences and conventions, all of which add up to the invaluable 'writers' grapevine' where you can exchange news and gather information.

If you do find an agent who is prepared to take you on, then find that the relationship isn't working, you are not tied to them for life. Discuss any problems you might be having, but if things don't improve you can move on.

First contact

This can be by phone, particularly if you just want to check whether that agent is still there and is currently reading submissions, but is preferable by letter. The process is similar to that of approaching publishers, described in the last chapter. The submission letter should be brief, stating the type of book you propose to write/have written and its word length; what special qualifications or experience you have to write it; your target audience; how your book has something new to offer in its field. You should also include a list of previously published work, if relevant, with the publisher and date.

Agents often receive complete autobiographies, lists of the author's pets, several pages on their computer's capabilities, and so on. This is not a good idea. An outline with chapter breakdowns as described in the last chapter should be enclosed although it need not be exhaustive. You might also want to include a sample chapter or two to give an example of your approach and style.

What happens next

If the agent is interested in the material and feels that she or he might be able to place it for you successfully, then they will want to take things further. Part of the agent's decision-making process is based on whether the author is planning more books, or if this is a one-off effort. Occasionally a one-off book will be worth handling, but an agent would be more likely to be interested in an ongoing career, an author they could help to build. They are probably also likely to be encouraged to hear that the writer intends working on other books in a similar field, rather than hopping from one area to another dramatically different one.

An agent may make suggestions about alterations to an outline or manuscript in order to make it more saleable and/or up to submission standard. Some agencies might be able to put a non-writer with a very saleable story in touch with a ghost writer. The only way to track down agents who can offer this service is to ring around.

If an agent is interested in *your* work, they'll give you a call or write, and you can begin to discuss terms. These are usually standard within agencies. All authors receive the same terms and negotiation is not an option. Some agencies have a contract with their clients laying out the services they offer, their commission and charges, and separation procedures, should it ever come to that. Others base their relationships on conversations, letters and mutual trust.

All UK literary agents used to charge 10 per cent commission on UK sales, but about a third are now, at the time of writing, up to 15 per cent. This is likely to become a growing trend as the cost of living increases. An agent is likely to have 'sub-agents' in countries overseas, who also receive a commission, so on translation deals, up to 25 per cent (15 per cent to the British agent and 10 per cent to the overseas agent) may be paid in commission. Where your agent sells direct to the publishers in the USA, commission could be 15 to 20 per cent because postage/phone rates to the USA are so much higher.

Commission is collected like this: the agent negotiates with the publisher to get the best possible advance, royalties and other terms, in full consultation with the author. The publisher pays the advance to the agent, who acts as a collection house on behalf of their client. The agent then deducts their commission and sends on the rest of the money to the author. The same happens with royalties. Some agents pay within a day or so of receipt, some wait until the end of the month. If your agent hangs on to monies for longer than six to eight weeks without any good explanation, think carefully. It's making interest in their bank account when it should be in yours. The Association of Agents lays down some general guidelines for agenting practice.

Some agents charge the author additional costs for expenses such as photocopying and postage. Some do not. Some agencies charge a reading fee. Some agencies reply quickly, others slowly. There is a wide variation, and it's a good idea to look out for an agent whose working practices suit you.

Once you have come to an arrangement with an agent, they will start to send out your work. You have now handed over the decision making to them, though they should be happy to discuss their methods with you. They will decide which editor(s) should see your manuscript or proposal first, whether to show it to several editors at once, how best to 'pitch' your project.

And remember that your agent has a private life too! Don't call in the evenings and at weekends without asking first, and don't panic if you don't hear instantaneously.

They may be ill, away on business or overloaded with work.

Clearly, you and the agent will both be hoping that the agent will get you a deal sufficiently better than you would have got for yourself to cover the agent's charges.

After publication

Once an offer to publish has been made and accepted, the agent will start to negotiate the contract. One of the main advantages of being agented is that you don't have to plough through the contract yourself. Agents understand publishing processes and are well-qualified to negotiate on your behalf.

If the agent retains certain rights from the publisher, such as translation or serial rights (that is the right to sell parts of the book to a newspaper or magazine), they will now begin to work on these. If your agent does keep such rights, it may be worth considering whether they or the publisher are best suited to handle them. If your subject is topical or controversial would the publisher have been better off handling serial rights as part of their publicity effort? How good does their rights department seem? Has your agent got you good deals abroad, or might your publisher have done better? Sometimes conglomerates who almost always work with agents aren't used to selling such rights, sometimes your publisher has a surprisingly good record in this area. It is always worth assessing the service you are getting from all concerned on an ongoing basis. Don't rock the boat unless you're sure there's a good reason – 'difficult' authors are often their own worst enemies. But keep an eye on things and ask for changes if you think them worthwhile.

You should now be developing a relationship with your publisher and the agent should step back to allow this to happen. But the agent should be available for the writer to ask questions and also, sometimes, to let off steam.

The agent may also be able to advise on how you can help in publicising your book, for example, on developing contacts with newspapers, radio and local bookshops.

And finally . . .

Remember that your relationship with your agent builds up over time. No two agents are the same, as no two writers are the same. If all is well, your agent should be calm and effective when all around may be chaos.

The legal side of publishing: Copyright and contracts
Lynette Owen

Every writer aiming for publication in book form should acquire some basic familiarity with the concept of copyright and the key elements which should appear in a contract between an author and a publisher.

Copyright is a property right which applies to literary, dramatic, musical, artistic and audiovisual works. It is regulated by legislation which defines the rights of creators; it also lists what uses can be made of copyright material only with permission of the copyright holder, and a limited number of uses which do not require such permission. In the United Kingdom it is currently covered by the UK Copyright, Designs and Patents Act 1988 which replaced an earlier Act of 1956. The 1988 Act contained many new provisions to cover developments in new technology which affect not only the forms in which copyright works may now appear (such as videotapes, computer programs, databases and multimedia works) but the ways in which copyright material can be exploited (by photocopying, electrocopying and the storage and transmission of copyright material electronically).

In the UK, a literary work is protected by copyright as soon as it is created; it is not necessary for the work to have been published in order for it to be protected by copyright, neither is a formal registration process required to secure copyright.

The first owner of copyright in a literary work is normally the author. The main exception to this rule is if the work is created by employees in the course of their employment, in which case the copyright will normally belong to the employer. Thus, staff journalists on a newspaper or magazine would not normally hold the copyright in their individual contributions, although a freelance journalist commissioned to write a special feature would normally retain copyright in the piece, unless there is agreement to the contrary.

Copyright grants authors economic rights, ie the right to receive a fair reward if the work is to be used commercially. The scale and form of that remuneration depend very much on the circumstances, such as the way in which the work is to be used, the status of the author and nature of the work itself. British copyright legislation (unlike the legislation of many socialist or former socialist countries) does not set any standard or minimum financial terms of payment for creative works; this is seen as a matter for commercial negotiation between creator and user.

The 1988 Copyright Act introduced fully into British copyright legislation for the first time a new concept which was already well established in European legislation: that of the moral rights of the author. These consist of two main elements: the right of paternity [sic] (ie the right to be credited as the creator of the work) and the right of integrity (the right not to have that work subjected to derogatory treatment, ie altered in a way which is detrimental to the work or the author's reputation). In the United Kingdom it is necessary for the author to assert the right of paternity and this is normally done by a statement to this effect printed on the reverse side of the title page of a book where other information such as the ownership of copyright in the work is normally printed. The publisher will usually add this automatically; the author should check that a paragraph to this effect is included in the book when proofs arrive. If it does not appear, the author should raise the issue and ensure that such a statement is included.

The UK Copyright Act also permits an author to waive the moral rights, something which might be requested by a publisher if the work in question is to form part of a larger work such as an encyclopedia where individual contributions might have to be cut in length or substantially edited to conform with the overall requirements of the work.

Under UK copyright law, the duration of copyright in a literary work used to be the lifetime of the author plus fifty years from the end of the year in which the author died; however, since 1 January 1996 this period has been extended to the author's lifetime plus seventy years to harmonise the period of copyright protection among the countries of the European Union.[1] Once the copyright period has expired, a work is said to be 'out of copyright' or 'in the public domain' at which point it can be used without permission or payment.

Copyright is a vital property right; if it did not exist, few writers or other creators would have any long-term incentive to continue since their work could be exploited by others for gain without authors being able to control such use or to receive any appropriate payment for the fruits of their labours. As the first owner of the copyright (except in the case of an employee work) the writer controls the right either to prevent the use of a work or to authorise others to use it in a variety of ways: through publication in the original language in whole or in part, publication in translation, adaptation of a novel into a stage play or a film, adaptation of a non-fiction work into a documentary and so on. The range of ways in which a literary work can be exploited will vary enormously according to the nature of the work and the status of the author.

When an author first seeks to have a work published, this may come about either through direct contact with a publishing house or via a literary agent. Agents tend to represent writers for the general market rather than academic authors, and choose whether or not to represent a writer. Many rely largely on the commission they earn from representing well-established writers, but they may be prepared to take on new writers if they feel they have potential, and may advise on the content and style of a work to make it more suitable for publication.

Once a publisher has expressed serious interest in a work, it is vital that the two sides are able to agree on a satisfactory contractual agreement to cover their relationship. While a deal may be sealed with a handshake, a good contract is nevertheless essential since it spells out the exact obligations of each party, how and when they should be fulfilled, the financial basis of the arrangement and provision for the arrangement to be terminated if appropriate. It has often been said that the indication of a good contract is that, once signed, it can be filed away by both parties and never needs to be retrieved in anger. It is therefore vital that the document is not only comprehensive and unambiguous but that it is perceived by both sides as a fair agreement. Agented authors, as well as those without agents, should have some understanding of the contract so that they know to what they have committed themselves.

There is no such document as a standard agreement between author and publisher although a number of models exist, most notably in Charles Clark: *Publishing Agreements: A Book of Precedents* (see the bibliography). In

1980 the two bodies representing writers in the United Kingdom, the Society of Authors and the Writers' Guild, produced Minimum Terms Agreements (MTAs) which sought to lay down basic terms for contracts between writers and users of their works, although such agreements perhaps refer most appropriately to titles produced for a general readership. They are not so relevant to academic writers. Relatively few publishers have adopted the terms of the MTAs exactly as they stand, but a number have adapted their own contracts to include most of the requirements. Although many basic elements should be common to all contracts, some details may vary considerably according to circumstances; for example, a contract for a new novel by a well-established popular writer may look rather different from that covering an academic monograph. A reputable publisher should always be prepared to explain the contents of a contract to a new author and to discuss any points which are of concern. The majority of contracts tend to follow a logical chronological sequence commencing with the rights which are being granted by the author to the publisher, a list of the tasks to be performed by both parties, details of the financial arrangements, a warranty and indemnity from the author to the publisher and finally provisions for the contract to be terminated in various circumstances. As contracts have inevitably become more complex over the years, a list of definitions of terminology may also be included.

The contract will normally commence with the date from which it is valid (usually filled in by the publisher either when the contract is first sent to the author or when it is signed by both parties) and the names and addresses of author and publisher as parties to the contract. It is customary for the contract to be applicable to the executors and assigns of the author (ie whoever is designated by the author to administer her or his estate, or a named person or company to whom rights in the author's work have been legally assigned) and to the assigns or successors in business of the publisher. This means that if a publishing house is taken over by another company, the contract will continue to be legally binding on the new ownership. In recent years there have been many changes of ownership in the publishing industry; if an author feels strongly that he or she objects to ownership being transferred in this way it would be necessary to build into the contract a requirement for prior consultation. However, the practicalities of consulting every author in the case of a change of company ownership tends to mean that only the most powerful established authors can successfully negotiate such a provision.

The rest of the contract will consist of a series of numbered clauses to cover detailed arrangements for publication of the work. The author will normally be required to deliver the text of the work (the length should be defined by an approximate word count) in an agreed form by an agreed date, together with any accompanying material such as illustrations, notes and appendices. It is vital that these instructions are clear (eg the number of copies of a typescript, the exact requirements for delivery on computer disk, whether diagrams will be supplied as finished artwork or as roughs to be redrawn). Many publishers now supply their authors with very detailed separate instructions on presentation and delivery. Since time is of the essence in publishing the contract may well specify that if the author fails to deliver by the agreed deadline (and if no extension has been separately agreed) the publisher may withdraw from the contract. If the author is unsure of meeting the deadline specified in the contract she or he will need to check with the publisher to see how flexible they will be on this point.

It is vital that a clear definition of the rights granted to the publisher appears at the beginning of the contract. It is here that the question of ownership of the copyright must be decided; in the case of works of fiction and popular non-fiction, it is common for the author to retain ownership of the copyright but to grant the publisher exclusive publishing rights for the work within an agreed territory, perhaps with the right to exploit additional rights such as translation rights. In educational and academic publishing it is quite common for the publisher to request a full assignment of copyright, although the contract should provide for the return of rights if the publisher ceases to exploit them actively.

Although authors may feel reluctant to part with ownership of the copyright, there are valid reasons for publishers in this sector requesting assignment. Educational and academic books are particularly vulnerable to piracy in countries with less than adequate copyright legislation and publishers have frequently embarked on long and expensive lawsuits to protect the rights of their authors and themselves. It is usually far easier to take action speedily and successfully if the publisher is clearly the owner of the rights. Another valid reason for assignment is where a book consists of contributions from many different writers.

If it is agreed that copyright will be assigned to the publisher, this will normally be for the full term of copyright (see page 165) with provision to recover the rights in a variety of circumstances. If copyright ownership is retained by the author, the contract will grant the publisher clearly defined rights for the full term of copyright or for an agreed number of years. The rights might be 'the exclusive right to print and publish the work in volume form in the English language throughout the world' or perhaps 'throughout the world with the exception of the United States and Canada' if separate publication arrangements are being made for those markets. The grant of rights in 'volume form' allows the publisher to produce the work as a complete book, either in hardback or paperback form, or both; any additional rights would need to be specified in the contract. The decision on what markets to grant should depend very much on the ability of the publisher to service that market either through a network of subsidiary companies or through distribution or sublicensing arrangements and any reputable publisher should be prepared to discuss how they will deal with key markets.

One result of the development of new technologies in recent years is that publishers may now wish to make arrangements to publish certain types of work in electronic as well as in traditional print-on-paper form, either themselves, in partnership with a software company or through licensing arrangements. This is a complex area and much depends on whether the publisher in question has the resources to exploit such rights if they are granted. Specific arrangements for payment for publication in electronic form will need to be agreed either at the time of contracting, or provision made for exact payment arrangements to be agreed between the parties at a later date.

The contract should spell out as clearly as possible the payments to be made by the publisher to the author and when those payments will be made. Arrangements may vary considerably according to the circumstances: for a book with a single author (or a small number of co-authors) a common arrangement would be an advance payment to be set against future royalty earnings from sales of the book. This means that after payment of the advance to the author, no further payments will be made until income from sales of the book have 'earned out' that advance. The size of the advance will vary according to the reputation of the author, the nature of the work and the required investment by the publisher, and the expected print run, price and sales. A small specialist publisher might not be able to pay an advance but might nevertheless be able to devote personal time and attention to the project and hence generate good sales and royalties for the book. Some kind of advance, however modest, is nevertheless welcome to seal the bargain. A larger publisher will almost always offer an advance, although in educational and academic publishing the advance may be modest for an untried author. It is increasingly likely that the advance will be paid in instalments – perhaps half on signature of the contract and half on publication, or perhaps one-third on signature, one-third on delivery and acceptance of the manuscript and one-third on publication. This 'staggering' of advance payments spreads the investment risk of the publisher but also provides the author with an incentive to deliver a satisfactory manuscript on time.

If a book has several co-authors there will normally be separate contracts with each one, specifying what share of the overall advance and royalties will be paid. For a contributed book, it is common for individual contributors to be paid an outright fee rather than an advance and royalties. This arrangement is normally covered by a short contractual letter; the overall editor of the work will probably receive a small advance and royalty. Although the payment of an outright fee for a single-author book was common in the nineteenth and early twentieth century, it is now relatively rare since it is recognised that if a book is successful the author should have an ongoing financial interest.

Royalty arrangements vary considerably according to circumstances. For many years it was common to pay an initial royalty rate of 8 to 10 per cent of the published price for publication in hardback form, and 6 to 7 per cent in the case of a paperback edition, with those percentages rising after an agreed number of copies had been sold. Many British and American publishers now prefer to calculate all royalty payments to the author on the sums they themselves receive since the discount granted to booksellers, overseas distributors and other purchasers such as book clubs can vary significantly. In addition, the collapse of the Net Book Agreement in October 1995 meant that most publishers will no longer set a fixed retail price but rather a recommended retail price on which booksellers now are at liberty to offer substantial reductions. Publishers operating on a sums-received basis may be prepared to offer a higher royalty percentage calculated on the sums received, eg 12 to 15 per cent for a hardback edition and 8 to 10 per cent for a paperback. It is important that if the publisher intends to publish in both forms (either simultaneously or with the paperback appearing later) royalty rates are specified separately, although income from both streams will normally be set against the overall advance payment.

Publishers who continue to work on the basis of royalties calculated on the UK published price will normally specify that the basic royalty rates apply to normal sales in the home market, but that royalties on any sales at high discount (often at 40 per cent or more) will be calculated on actual receipts. The contract will often specify that if the book is remaindered (ie sold to the public via 'remainder dealers' at a much lower price when normal sales have slowed down and the publisher has overstocks) the royalty will be calculated on net receipts unless copies are sold at less than the actual cost of production, in which case no royalties will be paid. If a book is remaindered, the author should be offered an agreed number of copies free of charge and the opportunity to purchase any remaining stock at a reduced price.

In addition to the financial arrangements for the

publisher's own sales of the book, the contract should specify any additional rights granted to the publisher and the payments due to the author from the sale of such rights. The range of rights to be granted should be discussed with the author before the contract is drawn up and here much will depend on the nature of the book and the resources available to the publisher to exploit such rights. If for example a UK publisher will not be distributing the book through a US subsidiary or regular US distributor, they may nevertheless be well placed to make arrangements for the US market through a licensing arrangement, either printing books on behalf of the US licensee alongside their own print run or allowing the US publisher to manufacture their own edition in return for an advance and royalty arrangement. If the publisher has no clear plans for the overseas markets and the author has the possibility of making separate arrangements, the territories granted to the original publisher should be tailored accordingly.

UK publishers will usually expect to have certain English language rights included in the contract; for example, the right to make arrangements with a book club (this may involve the publisher supplying the club with copies of the book at high discount, or perhaps licensing the club to manufacture its own edition in return for an advance and royalty). A publisher may also wish to have the right to license paperback rights to a paperback publisher if they feel this would be preferable to producing a paperback edition themselves. They may also want the right to authorise the book to be reprinted under licence in certain markets (eg a low-cost edition in a country such as India, which may result in higher sales than a full-price edition). Publishers may also request serial rights; these are the right to license the publication of extracts in newspapers or magazines either commencing prior to publication of the book itself (first serial rights) or after publication (second serial rights). Such arrangements tend to be for popular fiction and non-fiction titles and generate not only additional income but valuable publicity for the book itself if publication is carefully timed and controlled. First serial rights are often withheld from publishers if the author is well-known and represented by an agent.

The publisher will also expect to be able to grant permission to other publishers to quote limited extracts from the book in other publications; for all but the shortest extracts, a fee is normally charged. The publisher will usually control the right to grant licences for Braille editions and special recordings for visually disabled people. The publisher may also request the right to licence for commercial recordings and for the reading of extracts on radio and television. Full-scale film and television rights should only be granted if the publisher has the facility to exploit these rights, or if the author does not have an agent experienced in handling such rights and would not feel comfortable negotiating with film and television companies personally.

The question of whether control of translation rights should be granted to the publisher will depend on the resources available to the publisher. If they have an active in-house rights department (some small publishers employ a specialist agent for such sales) they may be best placed to promote the book to suitable foreign language publishers although there is never any guarantee that large numbers of rights can be sold. It makes little sense for an author to withhold such rights if there are no alternative means of dealing with foreign publishers but it is always worth asking the publishers what facilities they have to handle such rights.

The proportion of income to be paid to the author from each of the rights categories granted should be clearly specified in the contract. It is common for educational and academic publishers to pay the author a minimum of 50 per cent of such income and in some cases 75 per cent; although the range of rights which can realistically be exploited for such works is understandably more limited than for mass market titles, an active in-house rights department should work to maximise revenue from appropriate sources. For books with wider potential the percentage paid to the author may vary from 50 per cent for extract and anthology rights to perhaps as high as 90 per cent for paperback rights and first serial rights.

The contract should state clearly when the publisher will account to the author both for sales of the main edition and for rights income. Practice varies considerably; educational, academic and smaller publishers have tended to account once a year, calculating sales to an agreed date and making payment within an agreed period of that date (often three months). However, in 1995 a number of larger academic houses altered their policy and now account twice a year. Publishers of general books usually account twice a year. Some publishers account for income from rights sales as a separate item at the same time as they account for sales of their own edition. Others agree to pay out the author's share of any rights income as a separate item within an agreed number of weeks of receiving payment from licensees provided that the author's share amounts to more than an agreed practical minimum sum; if it is less than that amount, payment may be held over until the next normal accounting date.

It is important to be clear whether the author's share of any licence income will be paid out as a separate amount or whether it will be set against any outstanding unearned portion of the original advance paid to the author.

The contract will normally contain other financial pro-visions such as whether VAT will be added if the author is registered for VAT; a statement that any necessary tax will be deducted; and a statement of the currency in which accounting will be made. If the author is represented by a literary agent the contract will normally specify that all payments due to the author are to be made via the agent.

It is increasingly common for the contract to contain a clause covering the obligation of the publisher on whether to accept the manuscript once it is submitted. Publishers obviously do not wish to be held to publication if the work is either deficient in quality or if it does not conform to their expectations. It is therefore vital that an author has a clear brief at the earliest possible stage on what is expected in terms of content, length, level and style, and that there is regular contact between author and editor to ensure that the brief is being followed. Many publishers will insist on a clause enabling them to require the author to make changes to the work if it does not conform to the agreed brief; if the author declines to do so, the publisher will wish to be free to withdraw from publication altogether or to employ someone else to make the necessary changes, the cost of which will be set against payments to the original author.

There will normally be a general clause confirming that the publisher has full control over the general management of the work including design, production, promotion, pricing and sales, and the placing of subsidiary rights if these have been included in the contract. A good publisher will of course maintain contact with the author on progress of the work but it is usually only the most powerful mass market authors who have *contractual* control over aspects such as jacket or cover design, or where the book will be advertised.

Some contracts will specify that the publisher will publish the work by a specific date; others within an agreed period of acceptance of the manuscript; others within a reasonable period of time. It is important for an author to understand that large publishing houses have to coordinate production and publication schedules for large numbers of books; despite this it is not in the interests of a reputable publisher to unduly delay publication or to publish the book at an unsuitable time of year.

Since the introduction of moral rights into the 1988 UK Copyright Act some publishers may include in the contract a statement of the author's assertion of the right of paternity [sic] and may specify that the publisher should ensure that any UK licensees (eg a paperback house) should acknowledge this in their own editions.

The majority of British authors and publishers have agreed that their works should be included in the licensed photocopying system run by the Copyright Licensing Agency (CLA) and this may be referred to in the contract. The CLA regularly negotiates licences for limited photocopying of copyright material in schools and universities and is seeking to extend this to government bodies and private industry. Payment from photocopying licences is divided equally between author and publisher and the author's share is paid directly by the Authors' Licensing and Collecting Society (ALCS). Withholding a work from the scheme may simply mean that the work is photocopied and no revenue will be forthcoming.

It is a vital requirement that the contract includes a warranty and indemnity clause from the author to the publisher. In this clause the author guarantees that she or he has the power to make the agreement (ie that the rights granted *do* belong to the author), that the work is original and is not in breach of any existing agreement, will not infringe any existing copyright and that the work will not lead to any criminal prosecution or to a civil action. The clause will normally require that any outside material (text or illustrations) used in the work will be notified to the publisher and will either be in the public domain or used by permission of the copyright owners. There will also be a requirement to guarantee that the work is not defamatory or libellous (some publishers also require a warranty against obscenity) and that all statements purporting to be facts are true. The clause will require the author to indemnify the publisher against any loss or expense arising from a breach of the warranty. The publisher will often specify that they reserve the right to require alterations to the work if it is thought likely to result in a legal action (for example, a publisher might have a book read by a legal adviser for libel or obscenity).

This clause is a vital one for the publisher since they are the first target if legal action is threatened or brought for plagiarism, libel or illness or injury caused by inaccurate information contained in the book. Many publishers seek additional protection through taking out insurance, and a small number are prepared to take out insurance on behalf of their authors.

The question of whether any external copyright material owned by other parties (eg other publishers, picture agencies or museums) is to be included in the book is an important one and may be covered in the contract and through separate correspondence between author and publisher. It must be clearly agreed whether the author or the publisher will be responsible for obtaining permission for the use of such material and who will cover any fees charged (some publishers may agree to pay fees to designated level themselves; others may pay the fees but set the cost against payments due to the author). The inclusion of large amounts of external material, particularly illustrations, can add substantially to the cost of the book. If the author is to undertake the permissions clearance, the publisher can normally advise on the best form of wording to cover the rights required; some publishers will undertake the work on behalf of the author. In either case the publishers will often require that the clearance papers are lodged with them alongside the contract with the author.

If the work requires an index, the author will normally be asked to prepare this to specifications provided by the publisher. If for some reason the author cannot undertake this work the publisher may make arrangements for the work to be done elsewhere with the cost set against payments to the author.

The author will be required to check proofs of the work and to return them within an agreed time limit. It is common to specify that if the cost of author's corrections at proof stage (as opposed to correcting printer's errors) exceeds 10 per cent of the typesetting cost, the additional costs will be borne by the author. This is because authors are sometimes tempted to rewrite at proof stage, which is extremely expensive for the publisher, both in terms of time and resetting costs. Publishers will therefore discourage major rewriting at such a late stage in the production process, and will charge for any excessive changes. It is therefore important for the author to be happy with the final draft of the manuscript, although it is worth flagging to the editor if there might be any crucial changes necessary at proof stage (eg if there are major legal, technical or political developments imminent which might affect the content of the work and where updating could be important for the saleability of the book).

The contract should specify the number of free copies of the finished book to be supplied to the author and will normally allow for further copies to be purchased at trade discount provided that they are not for resale.

Publishers of non-fiction works will normally include a clause covering possible revision of the work at a later date. In some cases any new edition will be covered by the terms of the existing contract; in other cases a new contract will be drawn up, perhaps with a new advance and a revision of the royalty rates. If for some reasons the author is unable to undertake the revision (perhaps due to illness or lack of familiarity with new developments in the field) the publishers may specify that they may employ another author to revise the work and to adjust payment to the original author accordingly. This is particularly important in the textbook sector where a standard text may continue to be revised over the years by successive authors following the death of the original author.

It is vital that the question of termination of the contract is clearly covered since this may take place for a variety of reasons. If the publisher fails to comply with the terms of the contract or if the work is completely unavailable in any form in the original language, there should be provision for the author to give notice to the publisher for these circumstances to be remedied; if this has not been done within a reasonable period of time (eg three months) the author should give notice of termination and all rights will then revert to the author. The contract should not however terminate if the work is still available through a form of sublicensing such as a paperback licence or an American edition. Even if all English editions are out of print, the contract should specify that in the case of termination any authorised licences such as translation licences should be allowed to run their course.

Provision must also be made for termination if the author fails to fulfil the terms of the contract. Thus if the manuscript is not delivered by the agreed deadline or if it fails to conform to the agreed brief and cannot be revised to meet that brief, the contract will be cancelled and the author will normally be required to return any advance payment received. Once this has been done the publisher should return the manuscript and the contract will normally specify that they are then free to commission an alternative author to write the required work. Some publishers may however stipulate that if the contract is cancelled because the author fails to deliver the manuscript in time, the author has a continuing obligation to submit the completed manuscript first to the publisher on the same terms as those provided for in the original contract.

Some publishers may require that the author does not produce a competing work for another publisher during the life of this contract. Some may require that the author offers them the first option to publish the next appropriate work. Any such option should be for an agreed period of time following receipt of an outline, sample material or typescript of the work and should be subject to a separate contract on terms to be agreed.

The contract will normally provide for arbitration in the case of a dispute between author and publisher as the first port of call prior to embarking on legal action. The contract will normally be operable under the law of the country where the publisher is located. It must be signed by the author and by an authorised signatory of the publishing house; any subsequent changes must be in writing and signed by both parties.

While serious disagreement and legal action between author and publisher are rare, it cannot be stressed too strongly that the contract between an author and a publisher is an important document which sets out clearly the nature of the relationship between the two parties. A letter from a publisher to an author agreeing to publish a book may be taken as legally binding and in recent years judgement was made that a recorded telephone conversation between a publisher and an author also constituted a contract. However, such situations are far from satisfactory and a publisher should normally qualify correspondence and telephone conversations by stating that any commitment to publish is 'subject to contract'. The contract must however be freely negotiated and felt to be fair by both sides. Requirements by the publisher which may at first seem unfair to the author may be necessary for technical or commercial reasons which should be clearly explained by the publisher. The contract will remain a point of reference long after the book is published; it is surprising how many authors query matters with their publishers without referring to the contract which they signed!

Notes

1 Although this legislation came into force on 1 January 1996, it provides protection for those who acted in good faith in reliance on the previous period, including retrospective protection for all copies made before 1 July 1995 and licences of rights in some circumstances, but at the time of writing the exact scope of protection is not yet clear.

EDITING

Revising a first draft
Alex Bennion

So you have got to the end of your new book at last? The final sentence of the final chapter has been written, and you are feeling that glow of satisfaction described by so many contributors to this book just before the realisation sinks in that now the revision begins. Whether you are relatively new to writing, are on your first, full-length book, are new to non-fiction, or even have similar books under your belt, this moment is tough. Take a deep breath and remember all the advice you have been given – don't allow yourself to feel too discouraged, congratulate yourself on having come this far, take a break, have a holiday if you can – or at least a rest – and forget it all for a while. Do something non-cerebral if possible, that doesn't involve reading, writing or thinking. Do anything so long as it is not related to your project. Then you will feel refreshed and able to come back to the book with a new perspective.

It is a good idea to have some feedback from an outside eye at this point, and the best person is probably your editor, who has a vested interest in the project and its successful outcome. Don't try to go it alone without any objective criticism, unless you feel confident that you know exactly what you're doing.

On returning to the work, examine how you feel. Eager to get on with it? Or blocked and nervous? If the former, you will obviously have no problems in going on to the next stage. If you do feel at all blocked, this will need some careful handling. You had to address the issue of confronting that blank sheet of paper before you began your first draft, and the main hurdle has of course been overcome, but some additional factors may present themselves now.

Perhaps you feel worried, now that you are entering the final stages of preparing the book for publication, about how it will be received. Will the reviewers tear it to shreds? How will your friends and family react? If this is the case, try and reassure yourself and consider how important the views of other people, even eminent critics and experts, are to you. The opinions of other specialists in your field probably have some weight, so double-check all your facts and theories in order to feel as satisfied as possible that the work will stand up to examination. Then you can feel confident that you have done your very best.

What were your original motives for writing? Do you aspire to fame and glory, or would you rather shrink from the limelight, retain your privacy and stay invisible? Or do you worry that there will be no limelight, no reviews and that your book will be ignored? Whatever your anxieties, try and stay calm and hang on to the idea that your book will have intrinsic worth regardless of how it is received.

Perhaps you have other distractions and preoccupations that are preventing you from getting on with the task of revision. Try and clear these first and make some space – mental as well as physical – for yourself to work in. Do a little at a time, if necessary, even if you can only manage thirty minutes or an hour a day. Approach the exercise in 'bite-size' pieces, and say: 'I'll revise chapter one this week rather than aiming to get the whole book done.'

Giving yourself a realistic deadline can be helpful. The process does take time, but you can go on revising for ever and the text could become tired, stale and out-of-date. If you are hoping for perfection, accepting imperfection may be key – your work will never be definitively 'perfect'.

Re-read some of the other chapters in this book and try looking at other books available on the subject of writing for advice on dealing with psychological barriers and blocks. These works tend to be geared towards fiction-writing, but many of the factors related to this problem are relevant to writing non-fiction too. You may also find books on harnessing the 'right-brain' helpful, and some of these – as well as general books – are listed in the bibliography.

You were advised in the early stages of your project to prepare an outline that was as concise and detailed as possible. When approaching the first draft it was suggested that you should write – in contrast to the outline – as fully as possible, expanding and allowing yourself to think freely, so that new and potentially valuable ideas were more likely to occur to you.

Now compare your first draft with the outline. Have you missed anything out? If so, was this for a good reason? Have you developed any new ideas and areas? If so, speak to your editor and incorporate them with his or her approval.

I would look at a first draft for: a) the degree to which it conforms to the original outline (while keeping a flexible and open mind); b) any new and interesting elements; c) the general way it flows – are some passages rather laboured, forced, dull, long-winded, overwritten? Are there enough facts to back up your argument? Are some sections too short or long?

Let us say you are writing a book on nineteenth-century women's history in the UK, continental Europe and America. In your proposal you provided a chapter break-down that covered the following:

1 Industrial Revolution
2 French Revolution
3 Legal rights of women – divorce etc.
4 Women's rights over contraception, childbirth and their own bodies
5 Nineteenth-century society's attitudes towards woman
6 Careers and professions
7 The fight for the vote

You wanted to cover the whole of Europe, but haven't been able to find as much material as you had hoped (apart from the role women played during the French Revolution). So now you agree that the main focus of the book will be on the UK and the USA. This is appropriate for the market the book is likely to sell in, so your editor is quite happy.

Perhaps in your original outline you had planned to include a chapter on women's pastimes and domestic activities (housework, needlework and 'accomplishments'), but you now don't want to do this as you feel it risks perpetuating a stereotype. Your editor is keen that you should include the chapter and encourages you to look again at this area, as it would provide a more rounded portrayal of women's lives during the period. A process of negotiation ensues, and in the end your view prevails as you feel so strongly about the issue. There will be many similar instances in the course of revising the text, and an attitude of flexibility and compromise is essential on both sides.

Now the main shape of the work is there. Are there any passages that need cutting or expanding? Have you had difficulty in finding material in some areas, and do you have too much in others?

In writing the first draft you encountered some specific

problems, which you now want to address. You found plenty of material on the Industrial Revolution and the French Revolution, so you got off to a good start as far as content is concerned, though you need to edit it down and look at the style.

In the first chapter you discuss the violent changes of the Industrial Revolution, and the way in which women's lives were transformed from what you see as the comparative peace and control of pre-industrial times to the shattering horrors of life in the new factories and mines. You want to emphasise that the dramatic changes in women's lives following the entry of large numbers into the work force – together with the fact that among the new middle classes, who owed their wealth to the Revolution, it became a sign of prosperity for a man's wife and daughters to live in idleness apart from a little needlework and good works – had a profound effect, laying the foundation for the modern world and the various women's movements that arose during the nineteenth and twentieth centuries. However, you get rather carried away, go on at some length and the chapter becomes unbalanced and woolly. You need to cut this back for greater effect.

Turning to specifics in chapter two, you trace the role that women played alongside – and quite apart from – men during the French Revolution, and would like to give comparative examples from the American Revolution of the 1770s. The latter area was not included in your original outline as it falls outside the nineteenth-century period which you had originally agreed with your editor. But you now want to include the start of the Industrial Revolution too – the dates are hazy and all three elements mark an important transition into a new era.

Moving to the personal lives of women in chapter three, you talk of their property rights, their rights over their children and their right to divorce. A sorry picture emerges here, and you provide some telling examples. For instance, it was almost impossible for a woman to obtain a divorce during this era, even if there was clear evidence of her husband's adultery, cruelty and neglect, and you tell the story of Cecilia Cochrane, who in 1840 ran away from her husband to live in France with her mother. Her husband tricked her into returning to him, and then locked her up. The legal judgement was that 'there can be no doubt of the general dominion which the law of England attributes to the husband over the wife . . . [He] may keep her by force . . . he may beat her.'[1]

Quotes like this add life and emphasis to the points you are making, and you have a number of such stories. But there are so many that you feel you may have overdone it and need to find a way of balancing them. The techniques advised in earlier chapters come in handy here. Always keep your readers in mind and consider what they will find the most helpful and interesting, and remember that discarding is an essential part of the writing process – you can't put *everything* in. Reflect on whether you might have included too much detail and illustration and not enough factual comment and analysis. Are you sure that you have consistently linked your examples with the points you wish to make, and that your points are clear?

In chapter four you look at the key areas of contraception, childbirth and women's control over their own bodies. You are able to give the various elements of this subject appropriate attention, but feel on re-reading the chapter that the text is rather thin and needs fleshing out. So you return to your sources for more material.

In chapter five you turn to society's attitudes towards women, but find yourself getting rather bogged down and confused. Talking the problem through with your editor might be helpful, or you could try making a list of all the points you are trying to make, writing a summary of the material to try and get things clear in your own mind. What are you trying to say, and why?

In chapters six and seven you turn with some excitement to the strides women made in achieving a degree of parity with men in their careers and in their struggle to gain the vote. You end the story on a fresh note of hope (and with considerable relief!), looking towards the First World War and women's final attainment of the vote. Perhaps because you knew the end was in sight, these chapters work well and little structural alteration is needed.

Having cut and enlarged as necessary, you now have a balanced whole.

It is very important at this stage to check all your facts, references and quoted material, and to begin preparing your footnotes or endnotes now if you plan to have them. Not all books need them, but most works of non-fiction where the author has quoted from other books, articles or original source material should provide references. These do not need to be footnotes on the page itself, or even at the end of a chapter, but can all be placed at the end of the book, after the appendices if you are having any, but before the bibliography and index. You could call them 'Notes to the Text', or simply 'Notes'. If there are not many notes, you can put them at the foot of the page, using an asterisk for the first note and a dagger for the second. If you have more than two on a page, the numbering system is probably best, with the notes grouped at the end of the chapter or book. Notes can be numbered by chapter, so that the reader can refer to chapter 9, note 12, for example. This is a good way to avoid distracting the reader from the main body of the text, and it ensures that the work is accessible yet authoritative.

Your editor will probably have views about which system of reference is the most appropriate, but the usual method is to give author, title, publisher, date of publication and page references on the first mention. If the note immediately following is from the same source, use '*ibid*, p. 125'. If you refer to the same work several notes further on, provided that another work by the same author doesn't intervene, you can use 'Smith, *op. cit.*, pp. 16–18', or a shortened version of the title. Some publishers, however, advise against using *op. cit.* since few people know how to use it properly. Style varies, so it is worth checking your publisher's house rules in advance.

It is often a good idea to provide the reader with a list of further reading at the end of the book. You may not want this to cover every single work you consulted – this is probably unnecessary if not undesirable – and it may be best to call it simply Select Bibliography or Further Reading. You can group these by subject, chapter or simple alphabetical order (by author). Again, details of author, title (of both article and journal where appropriate), publisher (sometimes just place) and date of publication are needed.

Other matters to consider include appendices – which might, for example, include lists of figures or statistics – and illustrations. Will you be having any, and what form will they take: line drawings, diagrams, cartoons or photo-graphs? If picture research is necessary, will you or your publisher be responsible for this? Since illustrations are expensive to reproduce your publisher may have views on whether or how many illustrations should be included and what form they should take. This should always be discussed with your editor in advance. Remember to keep an eye out for any possible legal problems like libel or plagiarism – your editor will advise you on this.

Everything is now in place, balanced and checked. It is time to turn your attention to style. Like a sculptor with a lump of granite, you can begin gradually to refine the work and let it take shape.

Style is an individual matter, and you will want to find your own voice. But there are several basic principles to follow: simplify where possible, avoid repetition and irrelevance, and beware of over-ornate language. Check your grammar, punctuation and spelling, and consider consulting some of the many reference works available on English usage – such as whether or not it is permissible to split infinitives. You can also ask your editor if there is a publisher's house style for punctuation and spelling that you should follow. If you are presenting your work on disc, which some publishers now require, you should already have been given guidelines on the preferred formatting style. If not, ask now.

As far as the *tone* of the work is concerned, this may vary according to your subject matter, though you should aim for a fairly even emphasis throughout in terms of your presence as author. The subject has to come to life, but there is no need for your own emotions to intrude. For example, it is better to use quotes from the campaigning women of the time to express anger and frustration at the issues they faced, than to let a strident note creep into your own writing. Who could better express a woman's fury at the injustice of contemporary attitudes towards female 'inferiority' than Sojourner Truth, a black slave and abolitionist, speaking at a women's rights convention in 1851?

That man over there says women need to be helped into carriages and lifted over ditches, and to have the best place everywhere. Nobody ever helps me into carriages or over puddles, or gives me the best place – and ain't I a woman?

Look at this arm! I have ploughed and planted and gathered into barns, and no man could head me – and ain't I a woman?

I could work as much and eat as much as a man –

when I could get it – and bear the lash as well. And ain't
I a woman?

I have borne thirteen children, and seen most of 'em
sold off to slavery, and when I cried out with my
mother's grief, none but Jesus heard me – *and ain't I a
woman?*[2]

Of course, some aspects of your subject will be less
interesting to you than others, but if you are bored with
the material you should try to conceal it. Perhaps you
haven't fully got to grips with a certain topic: if your own
thoughts are vague and muddled, this is how the subject
will come across to the reader. Techniques for clarification
include the use of sub-heads to simplify the text, though
this should probably be done all the way through the
book; or tabular matter, charts and diagrams. And if you
feel that your readers' attention might waver at a certain
point, try varying the tone with an anecdote or example,
as I have done above.

Do as many drafts as you like, but remember to take a
break to stand back whenever necessary and show the text
to your editor for feedback if this seems appropriate. Avoid
doing this too often, though, or she will not be able to
perform the crucial function of standing back and looking
at the work from a new angle. It is fine to make amendments or depart from the original outline at any point (the
earlier the better), but it is a good idea to try and discuss
this first in order to avoid time and perhaps money being
spent unnecessarily. Your first instincts – about whether
or not to include something, for example – will often be
right.

Last but not least, you will want to consider what you
are going to have in the way of introductory matter.
Although an introduction and/or preface will come first
in the book, it may make sense to leave writing them

until the end, as you will then have a sufficient sense of perspective to be able to look back and introduce your book to the reader. If, however, you think it likely that you will feel too jaded by the end of the project to do this in a fresh and compelling way, tackle it at an earlier stage.

Your aim in a preface is to engage your reader's interest, so the subject should be presented in a concise and appealing manner, perhaps outlining what the book will cover and the approach you will take. If there is a controversial, new or thought-provoking element to this, now is the time to declare it. An introduction can be longer and more discursive, and you can ease into your subject in a more leisurely way. If you are going to have an introduction but no preface, this should combine both elements.

You may also want to include an acknowledgements page to thank the people who have assisted you – friends and partners, helpful librarians, experts in the field, and so on. It might be appropriate to include here a detailed list of acknowledgements to works you have quoted from (a precise form of wording is often provided by the publisher). Alternatively, these can go in the notes to the text.

You could add something by way of an afterword, though this is by no means essential and your final chapter may well be the best place to round off what you have to say.

At last the book is complete and the final draft ready for your editor. She may have further suggestions for additions, cuts, clarification and so on, so do be prepared for some additional work. But the more you have done at final draft stage, the less you should need to do later. Then the book is ready to go on to the copy-editor, typesetter and finally the printer.

You have created a unique piece of work which didn't exist before and is yours. You should feel proud of yourself.

Notes

1 Quoted in Rosalind Miles, *The Women's History of the World*, Michael Joseph, London, 1988, pp. 181–2, to which I am indebted for much of the background material in this chapter.

2 *Ibid*, p. 191.

Layout and design
Christine Pedotti Bonnel

Beyond laying out your material clearly, with sub-headings and so on, as discussed elsewhere, you will usually not have to worry too much about layout or design. This will be handled by the publisher's designers or art department. However, in some cases, your material will have to be shaped to fit a design and layout brief, for example in some heavily illustrated children's and adult's non-fiction. Here is one example.

A year after the publication of *Theo*, a French encyclopedia covering the whole area of Catholic culture – its Biblical roots, its history, the organisation of the Catholic church, its links with other religions, sacred art – the idea was hatched of revising this for younger readers. By the end of my first meeting with the publisher I had discovered how important commercial and financial considerations are in producing this type of book. I was forced to give in on the age-range – nine to sixteen rather than eight to twelve in order to increase the likely sales figures – and I lost 900,000 characters (that is, letters) out of the two million I had wanted (almost half the book). In return I got my budget and four-colour printing on every page.

My first editorial requirement was to make the book accessible to young readers, so that they could read it themselves without asking for explanations. The book was planned to meet the needs of two different kinds of reader.

The first has a specific question to ask, and so turns to the index, which therefore must be compiled with this in mind and enable her or him to find the right place quickly. The other kind of reader browses the book without any particular aim, so it is important to capture their attention.

I decided on a format where each topic was given a double page. This would allow the young reader to begin anywhere, wherever the book fell open. I also decided to make the index a substantial one, so that each key word would be defined briefly and each significant occurrence in the text would be presented in context. In the end the index comprised about a sixth of the book and became a readable section in its own right.

At this stage the content of the book was fixed page by page, or, to be more precise, double page by double page. Now the real editing business could begin. Here too there were more constraints, to do with the book's particular readership. Each double page had to be a self-contained world, and had to be readable without reference to what comes before. I also had to apply some basic principles of teaching: moving from what is known to what is not known, avoiding complicated or technical words, writing sentences with a simple grammatical structure. Apart from these general rules-of-thumb, my editing was dictated by the book's format. Each double-page topic was to be introduced and illustrated with a text of no more than 500 characters, and no paragraph could be more than 1000 characters long. Apart from the titles and sub-titles, there were six possible levels of text: the introduction; marginal text (technical glosses, tables, charts and definitions); quotations; captions for the illustrations; and the main piece on the subject, which I called the heart of the page, and which could be no more than 700 characters long. The whole came to an estimated total number of characters of between 5500 and 6000 per double page. Finding contributors who would be prepared to comply with these requirements was a difficult business. The space available for each subject was so restricted that it was necessary to select the information and arrange it in order of importance in a thoroughly ruthless fashion. Numerous specialists understandably refused to comply with these restraints.

It took a year of constant explaining, negotiating and rewriting to get together some twenty texts out of the 120 envisaged which conformed to my requirements. It was on the basis of this sample that work on the layout began. This threw up a fresh problem. In order to highlight the relationship between the original encyclopedia and the junior version, the format was reduced. If I still wanted a spacious layout for the text and to leave about a third of each page for illustrations, the text would have to be reduced by about a fifth, bringing the figure down to between 4500 and 5000 characters per double page.

From this point on, all work on the text was done in conjunction with the individual page layout. Illustrations comprised both newly commissioned drawings and requests to picture agencies. During the last year of work on the book, at the same time as commissioning, writing (I was an author too) and editing texts, I spent at least one whole day each week at the printers. I supervised the page layout, made sure the right priorities were assigned to the different levels of text, corrected the sketches sent in by the illustrators and chose the images (mainly reproductions of works of art) from those sent by the picture agencies.

Time and again, perfecting the final arrangement of a page would require making changes to the text. In order to accommodate the shape of a particular illustration the text would have to be recast: making one paragraph into two here, cutting a phrase there (or adding one) so that the page looked attractive. I also had to make sure that the titles were consistent and above all that the book remained coherent.

Despite all these editorial constraints and difficulties, it felt as if a book was being born. And by agreeing to be actively involved in the design and layout I kept the power to make decisions right to the end, and down to the smallest details.

Translated by Jeremy Thurlow

The copy-editor
Virginia Masardo

> Every author may aspire to praise: the [copy-editor] can
> only hope to escape reproach – and even this negative
> recompense has been yet granted to very few.
> (From Dr Johnson's *Preface* to his *Dictionary*)

Dear Author,

This chapter is to introduce you to the world of the
silent minority of publishing, that of the copy-editor. Low
profile, yet as indispensable to the process of your book's
production as the threshing machine is to separating the
wheat from the chaff, you will only meet us for a short
space of time.

It may seem to you that if you have produced a perfectly
typed script, with the requisite paragraph indentions, and
a friend has read it through for faulty punctuation or those
elusive literals (that is, typing errors), there should be no
necessity to send it to a copy-editor. Why should there be
any reason for anyone to tamper with your script, let alone
have it decorated with bright-red squiggles and esoteric
signs and crossings out? The first thing to understand is
that the copy-edit marks are not an indictment on your
material – that is not our brief. To use a tailoring analogy,
these marks, together with the designer's graphic 'mark-
up' of the layout, are the unpinnings and pinnings-up of
your creation, the markers for the machinist to follow, the

taking in and letting out for an easy hang and perfect fit. They aim to clarify the problems that could lead to production difficulties, neutralise potential obstacles between you and the reader, and to impose a visual structure thereby avoiding a haphazard outcome which would be expensive to alter after it had been machined. Our brief is to make sure it is complete and that it all works.

At the outset the copy-editor looks at how the material is presented. These days it makes a difference to the way the manuscript is treated whether it comes in as a conventionally typewritten 'script', or as a word-processed print-out, or electronic typescript (ie 'on disk'). Each method has its own set of possible problems. A little will be said about the electronic treatments here but much of that is trial and error, due to the idiosyncrasies of 'new technology' which is constantly evolving and advancing. Assuming for now that the author is using the traditional 'hard copy', the next thing the copy-editor will do, having assessed its shape and length – looking at whether it is straight text or whether there will be typographical interruptions such as headings, tables, figures and illustrations to fit – is to start reading the text with three different editing assessments in mind.

Editing for sense

Writers can become so 'close' to their manuscripts, that elements of obfuscation, contradiction or repetition can set in without their realising. Desk editors may have picked up much of this, but they focus more on matters of content and structure, leaving the line by line fine-tuning to us. Grammatical solecisms can surreptitiously intrude; perhaps two ideas have caused a problem resulting in the text not following on fluently in certain places or being unnecessarily repeated. There may have been difficulty over a choice of words and an unfortunate decision made. Any of these could cause your original meaning to become unclear to the reader while being perfectly clear to you. It is staggering the havoc a comma gone awry can cause, or the conundrums that evolve from the omission of a full point and following capital letter.

The copy-editor will also look out for factors you may either not know about, or have overlooked. For instance, potentially libellous statements; making sure copyright passages, sources, quotations, captions to tables and illustrations are correctly attributed; and that all data used is still relevant and up-to-date. Facts, names, and dates sometimes need to be double-checked, and a beady eye kept on slippery examples of unconscious bias, stereotyping, parochialism or 'political incorrectness'. It may be that the copy-editor feels an appendix, a glossary, or table of abbreviations would help the reader, and ask you to compile one. A fresh, impartial eye can spot the troughs: the copy-editor will be reading the text on behalf of your reader making sure it reads clearly throughout, and then coming back to you for discussion and confirmation on any points that seem confusing.

Editing for the typesetter

The copy-editor must also make sure the 'typescript', as well as being reader-friendly, is typesetter-friendly. This means that the copy-editor will mark up all the 'parts' of your book so that the typesetter will be able to identify them. There are particular marks and symbols, a code by which typesetters understand how to identify new paragraphs, heading levels, material which must be deleted, inserted, or moved from one place to another, and so on. These symbols are used to show how, for example, footnotes, illustrations, figures and tables, the index, or headings at the top of the page, should be laid out. Any problems that might arise with the layout of your book are pre-empted by the copy-editor's clear, unambiguous instructions to the typesetter and the path of production is smoothed.

Editing for consistency

Authors' intimate involvement with the content and tone of what they have to say often precludes attention to the more mundane questions of rules and printing conventions which, when applied to the mechanics or structure of a text, seal it with substance and credibility and are the secret to legibility. The name of the game here is 'consistency': in appearance, style and form. In this way the copy-editor 'marks up' a standardised treatment of the variables: special or optional spellings (-ize or -ise), capitalisation (President or president), abbreviations (Lt.-Col. or Lieut. Colonel), quotation marks (single or double), dates (the figure before the month or vice-versa), numbers (to spell these out or print them in figures), the style for bibliographical references (using the short-title or the Harvard system[1]). These choices, more often than not, are flexible and ones of personal preference. The cardinal rule, however, is that the copy-editor, having made the choice, is consistent.

House style

Many publishers supply their authors with a general 'house-style' guide to their preferred style for text, and bibliography and references system. Do ask for one if you are not sent one. A guide does not necessarily preclude you from having a word spelt or hyphenated the way you prefer, and if, having taken the house-style recommendations to heart, you wish to follow your own inclinations, this is fine, but be sure and make a note of them for the copy-editor.

Headings

The content of your text may require ordering under a series of headings and sub-headings. These have to be arranged typographically into a hierarchy of levels. More than three levels of heading – A, B, C – can lead to confusion for the reader and poses a problem for the designer. Where paragraphs are numbered, the same principle applies. Restricting your own ration of headings is a contribution to clarity.

Spelling

How do you spell the name of the busy shrub with reddish–purplish bell-like flowers – fuschia? fushia? fuchsia? What price seize or sieze, siege or seige, judgement or judgment, dependent or dependant, practise or practice, benefited or benefitted, focused or focussed? Spelling can be a jungle. Historical and orthographical reasons do exist for many seeming anomalies, which for the interested could provoke an intriguing foray into unexplored linguistic territory. Television credits and sub-titles, newspapers, advertisements, restaurant menus, are all great arenas for scoring unacclaimed victories in spotting errors. Next time you happen to be in front of the television when the football scores come up and you see 'Middlesborough – 1' you can score: wrong spelling – it's 'Middlesbrough'.

Words that have alternative or optional spellings, such as 'encyclopaedia' or 'encyclopedia', 'acknowledgement' with the 'e' or without it, 'inquiry' or 'enquiry', 'jailer', or 'gaoler', 'ageing' or 'aging', are too numerous to mention here, but if you are interested you will find a comprehensive list of these and typical difficult spellings in *Hart's Rules for Compositors and Readers*.[2]

Publishing houses can be nit-picking on questions of spelling. They can almost be divided into two camps: those who favour 'z' spellings (analyze) and those who are 's' spellers (analyse). You may be less interested. Gimlet-eyed copy-editors will usually nose-dive automatically into spelling errors, so don't unduly worry. But obviously your own awareness of spelling will make life easier for them. You should however be careful to apply consistent and accurate spellings to proper names and technical terms which the copy-editor may not know or be able to check.

The possessive apostrophe

Where does the possessive apostrophe go on 'Aristophanes *Clouds*'? Adding an apostrophe 's' to 'Aristophanes' here puts a euphonic strain on the combination. Try saying it. A couple of 'z' sounds are generated. It is better left off.

The 'its'/'it's' conundrum and the apostrophe-less '1960s', or 'NVQs' are common areas of error to bedevil the copy-editor's job. No matter how well versed we are in punctuation lore, we all tend to misuse these apostrophes on occasions.

Possessive apostrophes, like punctuation to dialogue, often become a grey area. If you are interested, you will find both *Hart's Rules* and Judith Butcher's *Handbook: Copy-editing for Editors, Authors, Publishers* (see Bibliography), comprehensive and helpful on both these points.

Hyphenation and punctuation

What are the odds on 'per cent' or 'percent'? 'proof-reader' or 'proofreader'? 'cooperation' or 'co-operation'? And what about 'north-west', 'North West' or 'North-west'? Well, it is anyone's bet. There is a growing tendency, as in other areas of modern life, for mergers. Contemporary writers on art or literature, for example, will use 'avantgarde' quite happily; writers on business or law flaunt 'abovementioned', 'decisionmaking', 'fundraiser' without any qualms. You may wish to be 'selfassertive' about your own views. Your feelings will be respected. But if you have a view, and want it taken into account, remember to brief the copy-editor by listing your requirements, and be as consistent as possible yourself.

Punctuation is a thing of changing fashion. Nowadays, in British publishing, commas enclosing clauses, commas and full points inside and outside quoted matter, full stops omitted from acronyms (USA), and after St, Dr, Mr and Mrs, Revd (not Rev.), but included after Cambs., will be taken care of by the copy-editor. Nevertheless you would do well to invest an on-going interest in punctuation changes if you are going to make a habit of writing books.

To Cap or not to cap?

The recipe for capitalisation is a mix of rule, preference and common sense. The growing tendency is to 'cap' as little as is permissible, particularly in headings. This is probably as much a question of aesthetics as anything. Capitals tend to clutter up the look of a page. Provided you make your wishes clear you naturally have the prerogative although you should adhere to the consistency rule. As ever, if you prefer not to have to worry about such matters, don't – it is the copy-editor's job to sort out these matters.

Discrepancies arise particularly in the use of words like 'court' and 'Court', 'church' and 'Church', 'Parliament' and 'parliament'. As Judith Butcher points out in her *Handbook* (p. 130), because capitals are used for the 'House of Commons', it does not follow that its generic associations like 'government', and 'prime minister' must also be capitalised. Of course definite rules apply to proper names, institutions, certain geographical names, titles, historical eras, political parties or movements, names of books, ships and so on. These are well covered in most books on grammar, and in *Hart's Rules* (pp. 8–14).

Italicisation and going **bold**

At the risk of being a spoil sport (or spoilsport or spoil-sport), and spoiling the fun you can have in tailoring your own scripts by indenting, reverting to small type, or making certain words italic, bold, or underlined for emphasis, it must be said that the cruel irony here is that this really is not helpful to the copy-editor. To start with, a line under a word is the typographical instruction for that word to be made italic in print. Your line might be redundant and have to be altered. In any event, avoid underlining for emphasis. If you let it, language properly used will do the job for you.

Where you can help is in the underlining of literary titles. *Hart's* gives you the low-down on these rules and on the italicisation of certain abbreviations and latinisms, and of the names of buildings, ships, and so on. There is also a full list of words that are commonly italicised such as: yes to *entente cordiale*, but no to aide-de-camp; yes to *raison d'être* but no to dramatis personae.

It is not helpful to produce your quoted material in italics as the copy-editor has to decide whether the quote should be 'run-on' in text, or displayed, and then mark it up accordingly in typesetter language. The rule of thumb here is that quotes of five lines and more should be displayed. Anything less, can normally be run-on in text.

The same goes for words to be set bold in print; the copy-editor will be identifying them typographically with the appropriate mark which is a squiggly line under the word. You may have emboldened for your own reasons which do not comply with print convention.

Abbreviations

For the sake of authenticity, abbreviations should be very carefully standardised. Verify meticulously, looking at cross-references and clarity of meaning to help the reader, particularly in words with scientific, medical, technical, literary, biographical or legal nomenclature. Inaccuracies lead to expensive corrections later on at 50 to 80p per correction (at the time of writing). It must be borne in mind that the copy-editor is probably not an expert in your subject matter and will rely on you for as much clarity in specialisms as you can give. Unfamiliar abbreviations should be explained or spelt out on their first appearance in text and thereafter abbreviated. Abbreviations in footnotes, and those which appear in text within parentheses (chap., pp., ll., *et al*, cf., *et seq*.), must be consistent.

Numbers and dates

Two rogue characters on the keyboard can cause hiccups. When you are keyboarding, watch out for the capital O (oh) which can be misleading to the typesetter if what you want is the figure 0 (zero). This is an area where you can help, particularly if your typescript is in a non-serif face (a serif face has short lines which extend from the stroke of letters). Typographically a zero with a diagonal line through it denotes its mathematical status (∅) and is easily identifiable by the copy-editor and typesetter. Similarly, the letter l (el) is often mistaken for the figure 1 (one), for example, where ll (el el) should read eleven (11) and vice versa. The capital 'I' meaning roman 'one' is another trickster. So are the minus sign (−) when confused with the em-rule (a parenthetical dash which is the length of the letter 'm'), and the multiplication sign (×) confused with the 'x' (ex). Again, it is the copy-editor's job to sort these matters out, although the more clearly you can present your material the easier the job will be.

The general rule for figures, if your text has a great many statistics or reports, is to spell out numbers from one to ten, while anything above that is printed in figures. Four-figure numbers do not always have a comma after the first figure (4000), five-figure numbers carry a thin space or a comma after the first two figures (45,000), while six figures are separated at the third digit by a thin space or a comma (600,000).

Your style guide will probably remind you that 'per cent' is spelt out in text, while % is only used with figures in tables or footnotes.

You have the option, when typing dates, of placing the day before the month (12 May, 1995, or 12 May 1995), or the reverse, American-style. It is not normal to print dates with the definite article (*the* 12th May), nor to use the preposition (*the* 12th *of* May).

Quotes

The rule a lot of publishers follow is single quote marks for quoted matter that crops up within a paragraph, and double quote marks for quotes within quotes. This is a sensible procedure and unless you have particular objections, or your text requires special treatment, it is a good rule to follow. If you are using a word processor, quote mark characters are often inadequately shown. You will become your copy-editor's invaluable ally by making quote marks visible and clear. Long passages of quoted matter that are 'displayed', rather than 'run-on' in text, do not need quote marks. The fact that they are displayed indicates quoted matter.

Always make sure, however, that quotes, punctuation, and spelling reproduced from an original text appear verbatim in your typescript.

Footnotes

— don't make them too long;
— be consistent in the use of abbreviations and punctuation (vol., ll., *c.*, ibid., (remember cf. means 'compare' not 'see'));
— present them on a separate sheet in one batch, double spaced;
— do not include complex notation and equations in footnotes;
— remember to change cross-reference numbering in the text accordingly when altering footnotes.

Tables

Large tables present problems with layout and you will probably discuss the pros and cons of splitting, or double-page spreading them with the copy-editor.

— send notes to tables, captions, figures and illustrations separately, and number them;
— make clarity of intention and relevance to context in headings self-evident;

— make headings concise and consistent, with minimal capitalisation and full points;
— mark clearly multiplication, addition and minus symbols; rules and dashes; decimal points; sub-/superscripts; mathematical and chemical notation.

Appendices and glossaries

— send these in separately;
— check that spellings, accents, abbreviations and ligatures tally with the text;
— pay attention to alphabetical presentation.

Bibliography and references

These details give back-up to your sources and acknowledge your reference to other people's work.

— establish the system to be used with the editor at the outset;
— check on cross-references: sections, figures, volume numbers, tables, chapters, and page numbers.

Lists

Technical and text book authors will probably need recourse to lists. The same restraint for lists should be used as for headings, sub-headings, and sub-sub-headings. They can be numbered, lettered, bulleted or given dashes. If you are unsure, the copy-editor will help précis them.

The WP

If your typescript is generated on a word processor, some of the traditional headaches for the copy-editor can be eliminated if you have been able to correct inconsistencies as you went along with your search and replace facility. But there are drawbacks. One of these would crop up in the shape of a gremlin or two if you had not standardised spelling or hyphenation *a priori*. For example, in globally changing ' –ize' to ' –ise', you could end up with 'size' becoming 'sise' all through the book.

Secondly, any revised copy or amendments sent in by you after copy-editing has begun, should be accompanied by clear marks indicating where alterations have been made, and a list of page and line numbers where amendments occur, so that the copy-editor can mark them in by hand on to their own copy. The reason for this is to avoid having to transfer the copy-editing work already done, on to your copy. It is possible that a whole new crop of minor changes may have taken place on the WP, requiring the whole page to be re-read.

Illegibility of certain characters on word-processed copy is another *bête noir* for copy-editors. Superscript and subscript characters (figures or symbols written above or below the preceding characters), accents, and quote marks can appear miniscule and ambiguous. It is helpful if the differences are made clear. In technical work, try to indicate whether figures and fractions are to be staggered ($^1/_3$) or aligned ($\frac{1}{3}$).

In mathematical equations and chemical structures, the similarity of some symbols to some Greek characters can give rise to discrepancies. They need attention.

Quote marks and commas, ligatures and accents – characters that can have an ambiguous appearance, need to be clear. If you do not declare your interests, the copy-editor may simply 'follow the book'.

The electronic way

With this method of text generation you will be handing over a disk together with 'hard copy'. The whole point to producing copy 'on disk' is to have done as much editing yourself with regards to standardisation and clean spelling, as to make production speedy and cost-effective.

It is possible the typesetting keyboarders will do the correcting themselves at the same time as converting the disk and 'interfacing' it to the typesetting machine without rekeying.

This is an option publishers are taking in increasing numbers as their vision of profit and efficiency overcomes residues of technophobia. The modern 'typesetter' (remember this is a machine! – of the utmost futuristic design and grace) works magic with the author's disk by 'interfacing'. This simply means that the disk is converted or 'formatted', so that it can 'talk' to the electronic typesetter and have it 'output' the material at a spanking pace, producing the article the copy-editor and designer tailored, and have it all ready as CRC (camera-ready copy) for the printers.

However, this method certainly does not eliminate a copy-editing read through the text for stylistic inconsistencies and standard of written material.

Moreover, watch out! Computer gremlins can get in here long before the printer's gremlin – the unthinkable and the unknowable can happen to electronic texts. So it is most important that you have a reliable back-up system, and that computer expertise is on hand to cope with the imponderables of 'viruses' and 'corrupted' data.

It is also important that a very close liaison be maintained between you, your publisher, the copy-editor, and possibly the human typesetter to make sure the right hand knows what the left hand is doing. It has been known at later stages in the proofing procedure of electronically-produced typescripts for whole passages to be found to have undergone strange metamorphoses along the way, or perhaps disappeared altogether, because someone, at some point, made an alteration unilaterally which was not communicated to the final printout. Technical work is particularly prone to this hazard.

Tables, footnotes or endnotes to go into electronic text, should all come on a separate file together at the end of each chapter, part, or section as the case may be.

Do's and don'ts

If you have time and interest while revising, think about the things in your typescript the copy-editor will be keeping a watchful eye on:

- that your argument follows, with no non-sequiturs, inconsistencies or contradictions and that there are no obscurities or ambiguities;
- repetition;
- over-long, unwieldy sentences;
- appropriate paragraphing;
- linguistic laziness, mix of style and metaphors;
- mad modernisms and comical neologisms for the sake of modernity;
- bad sentence construction and word order;
- bias, political incorrectness, parochialisms;
- doubtful word breaks (mans-laughter (manslaughter)), (leg-end (legend)).

Do

— preferably keep headings to a three-level minimum;
— identify quote marks, superscripts and ambiguous characters;
— number tables and illustrations and figures; and indicate their approximate position in text;
— check and brief copy-editor on cross-references, sources, abbreviations and bibliographical references;
— doublecheck dates and facts;
— be consistent with spelling, capitalisation, accents, hyphens, abbreviations and form of the possessive;
— verify and present clearly specialised nomenclature and terminology, and displayed formulae;
— brief the copy-editor on preferred treatment for footnotes or endnotes;
— discuss and confirm with the commissioning editor the organisation of the bibliographical and reference system to be used.

Thus far the story goes that whether typewritten, word-processed, or electronic your marked-up copy goes to the designer, thence to the typesetter, back to the publisher and here, historically, is your first set of first proofs. One copy of these will be returned to you for checking and another to the desk-editor – which is where the proof-reader comes in and we bow out. And unless anything rankly horrible happens in the interim, we will not see the typescript again.

Good luck, dear Author, with your finished book,
from the Copy-editor.

Notes

1 *Hart's Rules* are exhaustive on how to use references in a variety of texts and situations from poetry to law, to

unpublished sources and all types of manuscripts. The choice between use of the Harvard system of references and the short-title system is well covered in Judith Butcher's *The Cambridge Handbook: Copy-editing for Editors, Authors, Publishers*, pp. 251–8, 228–52 (see Bibliography).
2 The 1996 revised version of *Hart's Rules for Compositors and Readers* combines with the *Oxford Dictionary for Writers and Editors* in a concise usage and grammar section.

THE PUBLICATION
PROCESS

A view from inside
Moira Taylor

Writing a book is a creative act. Good publishing is a creative process, too, in so far as the publisher's duty is to ensure that the book reaches its widest market at the best possible time, looking maximally attractive and accessible to the people who wish to read it. In other words, it is the process of realisation of the book's essence and potential. Many people take part in this process but no matter how big the company or how prestigious, the most effectively run company will have small units and good communication and systems to ensure that production procedures are efficient and people are accountable for what they do. All the people who help to produce a book are interdependent with each other.

The academic publishing company I work for, employs 253 people and specialises in social science and humanities publishing. In smaller companies individuals often combine many of the tasks discussed below because the number of books published is smaller. In my first job in general publishing in New Zealand I edited typescripts, wrote promotional copy, organised marketing and publicity, and often took the author myself to the radio station to be interviewed. I looked after only 12 books a year. (It is now not unknown, however, for smaller publishers to be publishing up to 40 new books a year with staffs of under ten.) As a Senior Desk Editor in the UK I was responsible for between 40 and 50 books a year, most of them reference, textbook or additional reading on university courses from undergraduate to postgraduate level, and at any one time might handle 26 to 30 titles in various stages of production. Most of what I say here applies specifically to academic publishing, but the processes are, in varying degrees, the same whether in general trade or academic publishing. The single most important development in the last five years has been the rapid growth in new technology which has in some ways simplified and transformed systems and procedures, and in other ways created a climate of constant change and adaptation.

Personnel and processes

I like to think of the publishing unit as a wheel with the **commissioning editor** at the hub, commissioning the book, signing up the author in an appropriate contract, being accountable for the book's economic viability within its subject list and always moving outwards to assess future markets and publishing potential. The commissioning editor attends conferences and visits academic departments, looking at ways to improve the list, alert to new possibilities and changes in the world which will supply the raw material for publication. While nurturing new developments she or he will also be attentive to the existing backlist of books already published, ensuring those that should be are reprinted or produced in paperback at the appropriate time. If a book looks as if it will have a guaranteed student market and academics have shown interest in 'adopting' it on to existing courses as a text, then it is likely to be produced simultaneously in a dual hardback and paperback edition. The hardback will sell to the libraries at a higher price, the paperback to the student at an affordable price. The commissioning editor is the person to whom aspiring authors should write, sending a synopsis and sample chapter of the book they would like to see published and indicating the market it is aimed at, as discussed in previous chapters.

In a trade publishing house, whose products are directed at the general reading market, commissioning editors rely more heavily on agents to assist in the procurement of new books and the signing up of authors. The decision about whether to publish in paperback as well as hardback depends on whether there is a general library readership or whether reviews in the prestigious national press are crucial to the book. (The national papers are very reluctant to give good review space to paperbacks.)

Linked together around the commissioning editor are all the people who liaise together to produce the book. The **editorial assistant** (in some companies, a secretary or assistant editor) assists the commissioning editor to function. The assistant and editor between them ensure that the contract is signed, the typescript in on time, the illustrations in, the permissions for use of borrowed text or illustrations acquired, the draft blurb written and the author's personal details obtained. It is usually the editorial assistant who, directed by the commissioning editor, sends the typescript out to selected readers for reports on the quality of the text and its suitability for specific markets.

Once the editorial assistant has assembled all the essentials relating to the finished typescript and the commissioning editor is satisfied that it can now be produced it is passed to the **desk editor**, the person who shepherds the typescript through its production process from typescript to finished book, ensuring it is copy-edited and proofread by the appropriate people (in some companies the desk editor herself) and in a fit state to be published. Desk editors liaise directly with the author about the cover, the production process, the copy-editing or proofreading processes, ensuring that the author knows what his or her responsibilities are.

The first job of the desk editor is usually to write an introductory letter to the author/editor, outlining the future production process and schedule, often naming the key marketing person who will be handling all matters relating to the reviewing of the finished book and the advance marketing and promotion of the book-in-progress.

Once the typescript has been copy-edited and typeset and page proofs are available, a **proofreader** reads the proof against the copy-edited manuscript to ensure that all editorial corrections have been made and to correct any mistakes made by the typesetter. The author will also be sent a proof by the desk editor and, once marked, this proof will be collated with the proofreader's before being returned for correction to the typesetter. A second revised proof will usually be checked in-house by the desk editor or staff supervised by her and, finally corrected, will return to the desk editor as camera-ready copy, which should be error free. If an index is necessary, this is compiled – either by the author or by a freelancer – at first-proof stage.

The desk editor will sometimes be involved in refining the book's blurb and submitting it to the author for approval before finalising its form for marketing and promotion purposes. Sometimes this is handled entirely by marketing or publicity personnel. Copy on the paperback cover or jacket of the book is sometimes the desk editor's responsibility, sometimes that of publicity, and in some cases, a separate copy-writing department handles the copy. As the design of the cover is finalised and copy and design merge, the cover will return to the desk editor several times for checking during the course of its production. During the time the book is being produced, she or he will liaise with the author and all others involved to ensure that every stage of the editorial and production processes are completed as well as possible within a scheduled time.

The **production controller** organises the typesetting, printing and binding of the book, liaising closely with the desk editor to ensure deadlines are kept, and looking for the most appropriate company to do a particular job. Some typesetters will be highly skilled at dealing with author's disks; others, less skilled in computer technology, might have particular strengths in text design or be superbly equipped for originating illustrations. The production controller becomes adept at manipulating suppliers (typesetters/binders/printers) according to the schedules that must be kept. A production controller will often be asked by a commissioning editor to supply advance costings and sample pages on the production of a particular type of book before the production process begins. She or he will also estimate the length of the book, calculated from the size of typeface used in the body copy, the size of different headings and the amount of space allowed for illustrations and other parts of the book, then produce a specification for the typesetters to follow. The other key part of the production controller's job is to negotiate the best possible prices for printing, typesetting, paper supplies and so on. The production role is crucial in keeping publishers' costs to a minimum.

(Since writing the first draft of this chapter, the roles of the desk editor and production controller within the company I work for are in the throes of radical change, reflecting the advance of new technology and the need to retain position in the constantly changing marketplace. Desk editors are extending their functions to include liaison with typesetters, and the application of type specification detail to typescripts, while retaining liaison with out-of-house freelance editors and proofreaders and author contact through the production process. They are becoming 'production editors'. Production controllers, while still retaining contact with the printing and binding suppliers, are training in on-screen editing and will provide edited manuscripts on disk for eventual page makeup in-house. All commissioning editors are thinking of add-on electronic products to enhance their academic books where appropriate and ensure they retain their competitive edge. Journal editors are exploring the Internet as a possible route for contributors and subscribers and 'home pages' are firmly established on the Internet as an additional form of advertising.)

The format and design of the interior of the book are usually decided by the commissioning editor in consultation with designers, the desk editor and production controller and are dependent on the expected market. A high-profile book is more likely to have extra money spent on design. Textbooks, with a higher life expectancy than other course books, need clarity of design and layout if they are to be consulted day after day by students. If a book is highly illustrated and the relationship of text to illustration is vitally important, pages are set first in galley proofs or unpaginated pages, so that the desk editor and designer can cut and paste a chapter to suit without causing costly repagination.

Typesetting today is far removed from the hand setting done by Virginia Woolf when she set Katherine Mansfield's short stories and T. S. Eliot's *The Waste Land*. Typesetters are turning more and more to desk-top publishing systems (DTP) for page make-up, 3B2 and Quark being the preferred tools used by the suppliers of the publishing company where I work. Data capture tends to be one of three options: re-keying copy; using author's disks; or scanning. If the book is not on disk, a typesetter will give the typescript to a keyboard operator who will key onto computer up to 120,000 keystrokes in a day (20,000 words in six hours). There is an increasing tendency to send material abroad where keying is very cheap; popular destinations are Mauritius and the Phillipines. Or, using author's disks, the typesetter will incorporate all the copy-editor's editorial corrections and add formatting codes for headings, etc. into the document at the same time. Sometimes a manuscript may be scanned (photographed) using optical character recognition (OCR) scanners and software which converts it to text which is saved as a word-processed file. (Occasionally the publisher will accept camera-ready copy directly from an author, ready for printing, but it doesn't normally have the refinements of the copy-editing and editorial processes and this is usually obvious to a discerning reader.)

The publishing house I work for is in the process of changing from a system where the text is output initially as high-resolution laser output on plain paper – the proof – which is photocopied for the author and proofreader to read, and later at revised (corrected) proof stage output as bromide (camera-ready copy), to a system where the final output is in the form of postcript files, that is, a floppy disk, which will then be sent to a printer to make film/plates. Printers tend to use either web printing presses, like those used to produce newspapers, or sheet-fed presses.

The impact of computerised technology on the typesetting and printing process has been huge. It has meant typesetters can produce much more than before and more quickly. Suppliers are resultingly more flexible about what they are able to do. Typesetting prices have fallen dramatically. Ten years ago a Royal format page would have cost £5.50 to typeset; that same page today can be typeset for £3.00 to £3.50 and sometimes less. Following a period of rapidly increasing paper costs, these are now more stable. Occasionally the progress of a book will be held up by an order for a specific type of paper which needs to be manufactured specially for the job.

The **cover design** is naturally a vital part of the book's production. The cover or jacket of the book is what the bookseller and the book buyer first see. In a perfect world, the book's cover copy describing the contents and the author's details should be enhanced and reflected by the cover design so that the book shouts 'Buy me!' to its potential market. To make the designer's job easier, the commissioning editor provides a 'design brief' outlining the market potential for the book, the essential subject area covered and the type of cover which is desirable. This and the blurb gives the designer the raw material. In some publishing houses, the commissioning editor will suggest or provide a particular image (photo or line drawing) for use on the cover. In others, an illustrator is commissioned to provide the image.

Designers, in some companies now proficient in computer-aided design, have to work within restrictions provided by the amount of text copy, usually some form of logo or design pattern which identifies the company in its market, the length of the title, sub-title and author's name, which must be featured on the front and spine of the cover, and a certain number of colours, between two and four, already decided by the estimated price of the book and usually laid down in the design brief.

One of the greatest sources of friction in a publishing house can be between designers, who like to exercise the freedom of their imaginations, and the editorial and marketing teams who sometimes insist on reining in the designer's fancy. Sometimes a design much loved by its creator does not reflect the content of the book or will not appeal to the target market according to editorial and sales personnel. The design brief given to the designer by the commissioning editor should minimise this, but often it doesn't. The designer will usually provide a cover 'rough' – a sketched model for the cover showing layout and colour. Ultimately, it is usually the commissioning editor who decides on the final design since it is she or he who knows the book in detail or what the market requires; although in some – usually more mass-market – companies, key members of the sales team have the final say based on what is or isn't a 'selling jacket'.

Authors often like to have a say in the cover design but this may meet with resistance because they may not know what will succeed in a particular market. Sometimes a designer will consider and skilfully adapt an author's design idea but generally academic publishers are careful to retain all rights in cover production so they are not hamstrung by an author with designer proclivities. More general publishers vary in the extent to which authors are given a say on their covers.

Marketing and promotion of the book begin as soon as the draft blurb describing the books's contents and its author is written. The blurb is usually the tool of the **marketing director** or **marketing controller** who uses it in various forms to promote the book, whether in advertisements, in seasonal and/or specialist catalogue copy, or in marketing leaflets distributed at conferences and any gatherings where large numbers of potential buyers congregate. In academic publishing, the marketing controller liaises directly with the author to ensure that all possible sources of interest are covered and to anticipate when likely conferences may occur so that the book can be well represented there in advance publicity. In more general publishing, authors have varying amounts of liaison with the marketing staff, from none at all, to regular discussions.

Once the advance copies of the book arrive, usually from two to six weeks before publication, the marketing controller creates a review list of special journals and national media to which review copies are sent. It is important to include known 'names' in the field of interest so that favourable review quotes can be elicited which can be used to promote future sales of the book. No matter how beautifully written an academic blurb is, the effusive recommendation of an authority in a specialist field will always carry more weight to the potential reader. Marketing personnel have access to databanks with every known journal or magazine in a particular field of interest. They soon build up personal know-how in their list areas.

If a book is expected to create wide media interest outside a specialist area, the **publicity manager** is engaged to plan a publicity campaign with press releases and sometimes a 'launch' at a suitable venue on publication day to which the national press, radio and television are invited. Personal interviews with the author are arranged. Books are highly selected for this treatment and usually have some topical or controversial interest at the time. The cost of a launch precludes giving this push to all published books, much to the chagrin of some authors. Academic publicity managers will be keen to promote titles which will be of interest outside the academy as well as inside. They can be books giving a new angle in research, or touching on issues in current debate; or controversial or provocative books, which will encourage discussion. Academics with a reputation extending beyond the academy – Karl Popper or Jacques Derrida, for instance – are likely to be good to promote. Ideally, the book will not be too specialised and will be accessible to the journalists and unacademic readers. It might also tie in with outside events. An important part of the selection of a title for publicity will be the author. Is she or he UK-based and available for a publicity campaign? Can she or he *talk* under the glare of television lights or, more likely, in response to an interrogation by a radio or newspaper journalist? (For a more detailed look at publicity, from a more general publisher's perspective, see Karen McCarthy's chapter.)

Preparation of the author and the typescript

The author needs to be prepared in submitting the typescript so that it is as complete as it can be, and in a form which will ensure the publishing process is as painless as possible for everyone concerned. These days, certainly in academic publishing, that often means disks. In these cases, as soon as the contract is signed with the commissioning editor, the author is sent an instruction book requesting that the typescript is prepared on a word processor, using double-line spacing so editors have space to insert their corrections and markings and with wide margins (3 to 4 cm) on both sides as well as at the top and bottom of the page. It must be prepared on good-quality paper using one side of the page only. Two copies of the typescript are necessary, one for keeping in-house as an insurance if the other goes astray in the post when it is sent out to a copy-editor. Or it may be necessary to send a copy of the typescript to a book club for assessment or to a text designer if it is to have special treatment. All copies sent in by the author must be identical: the typescript must be an exact printout of the disks sent, and it should be dated.

Commissioning editors ask for a certain **length of typescript** – so many thousand words – because they know exactly the length of book they can ensure will sell in a particular market. Many wordprocessing packages include facilities for automatic word counting and it is helpful if the author notes the number of words on the front of the typescript or for individual chapters as they begin. One of the headaches for many authors is the problem of ensuring that the book conforms to the approximate word count. In collected editions, where contributors are submitting chapters, often from different parts of the world, the temptation is to accept the submission without alteration and eventually find that the book has grossly exceeded the requested word count. Extra pages mean extra cost and if the price of the book has to rise it may price itself out of its intended market.

Typescript pages must be numbered just before submission, when the organisation of the book is complete and all figures and tables have been included. Because the publisher will be adding the company's own additional pages to the preliminary pages, the numbering should begin with the first page of the text and continue until the last page, not chapter by chapter. The author should ensure that all copies are numbered identically. This is important because at a later stage when editors are asking specific questions about the typescript, it is important that everyone involved is consulting the same page.

The **title** chosen by the author may sound wonderful but it may not adequately satisfy the commissioning editor's idea of what the book is about or the sales and marketing departments' notion of how well it conveys the message of the book to its market. Authors should not be surprised if the title changes, after consultation of course, and if a sub-title is added which complements and extends the original title. It is amazing how frequently titles are repeated. The title must distinguish the book singularly within the publishing house and also out in the marketplace. *Immortal, Invisible* is a lovely and poetic title for a book on films made about lesbians but it doesn't convey that information without its sub-title: *Lesbians and the moving image.*

One of the most essential resources accompanying the typescript and requested by the commissioning editor at the time of submission is the **Author's Questionnaire**. This asks a mass of questions about the author's career to date, what he or she thinks the book is about in a few concise paragraphs, who is seen as the potential competition, in which specialist journals and publications the author would like to see the book reviewed and, if it is a contributed volume, the names and addresses of all the contributors. Overworked academics and authors often feel despair when confronted with such a document after the creative fire has died down and the typescript is ready for delivery, but it has to be done. It provides the raw material for the next major stage of the book's life – its ongoing marketing and promotion.

The polishing of the typescript

It is essential that a book is able to be read as easily as possible. One of the processes which may not be visible to the reader but which would be immediately apparent if the published book were to be compared to the original typescript, is the copy-editing which ensures that punctuation is correct, sentences are grammatical and spelling correct, conforming to either the English conventions if the book is written by an English author, or American if that is the case, and generally querying with the author any factual anomalies or inconsistencies and omissions in referencing (see also Virginia Masardo's chapter). This is particularly difficult if, as is often the case in academic publishing, in a collected edition there is an assortment of both English and American contributors or even German, Scandinavian and Japanese, all in the one volume. It is the job of the controlling editor, who gathers the contributions together before submitting the manuscript to a publisher, to ensure that the book has one style of spelling, punctuation and referencing but often hard-pressed academics are unable to do this and then the tasks of the desk editor and copy-editor are crucial: the first in establishing which style to follow and briefing the copy-editor to ensure that this is achieved, the second in carrying out the task within the budget defined by the desk editor. Desk editors draw on a pool of freelance copy-editors whose strengths and weaknesses are well known from previous work done. They have particular subject strengths whether in literature, philosophy, classics or individual languages, for instance.

Costs

Today, when there is such a variety of books on the market and readers have become highly selective, the retail price of the book is a critical factor in its success or failure. Every detail of cost from copy-editing, design, proofreading, in-house freelance help, typesetting, printing, binding, marketing, paper costs and a contribution to the company's overheads – heating, lighting, staff costs, equipment, and so on – are estimated before the book goes to production. Everyone involved strives to keep the book within its proposed budget, which is calculated on the estimated extent of the book, its print run (number of copies produced) and expected market. Once most costs are known and the book is in its final stages of production, a final reckoning is made by the commissioning editor and a final price fixed. This is passed at a meeting where other commissioning editors as well as marketing and sales representatives are usually present to offer advice and caution as well as enthusiasm.

Authors may assume that there is a pot of gold into which the publisher dips when unusual expenses arise in the production of a book because, for instance, the author has not produced usable illustrations, or because sudden translations need to be made or additional editing needs to be done. Unfortunately this is not the case. Most, if not all, expenses are charged to the book. Publishing is a labour-intensive industry and an academic book will reflect the high cost of production, particularly because the print runs are small compared to more popular books sold in the trade market. Print runs can vary from 500 for a hardback monograph to 5000 for a student paperback, and the high cost of production is felt intensely in the retail price which can be up to £75 for a highly illustrated hardback of up to 800 pages but averages at between £35 and £40 for most hardbacks and between £8.99 to £14.99 for paperbacks. But who is going to buy the £75 hardback? Not the student, for whom that money is more than a week's rent. If the book is a text book she or he will buy the paperback to carry them through the course. No, university libraries are the principal purchasers of the hardback edition. For general publishers, prices have to be kept low, so that ordinary readers will be able to pay for the book. Unless the book in question is clearly a best-seller, general publishers also have to work very hard at keeping costs low.

Advent of the finished book

Much rides on this. The day the book is due in from the binder can be nerve-racking for everyone. After all no one knows what the book is going to look like. Some massive problem may not have been avoided at the printers, whose staff are recovering from a 'flu epidemic. Several hundred books may have pages 50 to 85 printed upside-down. The top margins of the book may be twice the appropriate size because the desk editor's lover deserted on the day camera-ready copy arrived and she had other things on her mind. The production controller, in a fit of pique at the incessant harrying of the desk editor, may have stubbornly refused to remove the blemish from a key illustration because she couldn't face the delay and cost in reorigination. Whatever has occurred in the preceding six months, whatever sleepless nights may have been spent over the book, the hour of reckoning is at hand. Desk editors can usually tell from the facial and body language of the production controller bearing the book whether joy is called for or rage and despair. If there is a dreadful mistake, the publishers may have to pay substantial amounts of money to have it corrected, or live with the error as it is. Explaining the former to one's boss or the latter to one's author is not a pleasant prospect. If the error is the printer's, the publisher may not have to pay, but valuable time can be lost. The desk editor pours over known or suspected problem areas before admitting gratification. There is a particular look which comes over the face of a desk editor examining a finished book: studied apprehension.

Once the book has been bound, advance copies are sent to the publisher while the rest are stacked at the company's distribution centre, ready to be sent out to book shops to be on sale by the publication date. The author is sent an advance copy and further copies can be ordered, depending on the number due to the author by contract. Orders or 'dues' have by this time built up on the sales database, recorded from individual orders made by bookshops, customers attending conferences featuring advance publicity of the book, or by customers reading advance publicity in catalogues. Some eventual orders will be the result of customers receiving inspection copies from the publisher on a sale or return basis.

The future

Publishing has been thrown into a ferment by the advent of electronic publishing and the almost instantaneous global communication possible through the Internet and electronic mail. Are we now the global village predicted by Marshal McCluhan 25 years ago? Will books disappear? As publishers scramble to get space on the Internet and think of how best to acquire a market share of the new types of products and services possible through electronic and telecommunications technologies – electronic texts, multimedia projects, catalogue coverage and customer service via the Internet – writers continue to craft words into digestible, exciting and provocative forms. Publishers will survive whether producing books or electronic products but the path their future will take is an open question.

Publicity
Karen McCarthy

At last! Your manuscript is complete; the seemingly endless editing process is over; you have even read and returned your proofs. At this stage it may seem as if your work is done and that your role as an author is drawing to a close. However, whether you see it as good news or bad, this may not be the case. Appearing on television and radio, talking to newspaper and magazine journalists, travelling around the country on author tours are all ways in which you might be able to work towards making your book more of a sales success, certainly within general publishing.

Publicity is a key stage in the publishing process: it is the point at which the public will be made aware of you the author and your work. This is the time when people can discover not just that your book exists – but also that they will want to read, and ideally, buy it.

Thousands of books are published in Britain every year and the majority of these are non-fiction. Figures from Whitaker's Database show that in 1994 new non-fiction titles outnumbered new fiction by approximately three to one, with this ratio continuing through the first half of 1995. As review copies of a high proportion of these new books are sent in to national broadsheet literary and features editors, space is very limited and competition for coverage is fierce.

Natasha Walter, who was at the time of writing, Deputy Literary Editor at *The Independent*, receives approximately 50 books a day, yet only a handful of these will be reviewed or featured: 'In terms of the number of books published what we're actually able to cover is the tip of the iceberg – less than 10 per cent of books sent in get reviewed – there simply isn't the space.' At *The Independent* non-fiction coverage hovers between 40 to 50 per cent – with biographies and literary non-fiction getting the larger share of that space.

The publicist's role is to convince the media that you, your book and the issues it covers are newsworthy enough to write about. In a sense publicists act as translators: with non-fiction their job is to transform what may well be a detailed and in-depth work in a specific subject area into something that will be taken up by the media as broadly understandable to a wide and varied readership.

Non-fiction titles will usually have their own niche, however obscure the subject may seem, but even the most specialist work can have topical angles which will interest the mainstream media. For example, a critical analysis of the work of George Eliot will attract different specialist media coverage to a book about great women explorers, or a practical self-help guide on dealing with emotional or relationship issues – but at the same time all three might be reviewed on a general books page of a monthly magazine.

Newspaper and magazine editors, staff and freelance journalists, radio and television producers at a local, national and specialist level will all be contacted by a general publisher's press office on a regular basis.

Reviews, author profiles and interviews, feature articles, and guest appearances on television and radio are the most common forms of media coverage. Sometimes a book may even prompt a news story, which can dramatically raise the profile of both the book itself and the issues raised in your work. Recommendations by advice columnists and feature writers, competitions and promotional give-aways are other types of exposure a book can attract.

Features editors will be interested in hearing about new non-fiction books – particularly if your subject ties in with a topical issue or current news story. Coverage could be a passing reference in a feature article, or possibly an extensive interview or profile. One of the few times when it is more appropriate for an author to approach a publication direct than via the publisher would be to discuss the possibility of contributing a feature article as a journalist. Preliminary contact could be made by the publicist or even your agent if you have one, any follow-up in this case may be best coming from you, so that you can talk the editor through the piece you have in mind. Writing an article could help raise the profile of the book and enhance your reputation as an expert in the field.

But before approaching any of your contacts directly do speak to the publicity department first and let them know what you have in mind. If, for example, the publishers are looking to sell serial rights to your unauthorised biography of a controversial public figure to Sunday newspapers or supplements, then a call from the author offering to write an article instead could be confusing for an editor – and undermine the work already done.

Keeping the publicist up-to-date on any ideas or useful contacts which you have will also help ensure that wherever possible you are projecting professional consistency to editors and journalists. Developing a co-operative professional relationship with the publicity department facilitates the publicity process and helps maximise a book's potential.

Some publicists establish early contact with writers either by fax or phone or by suggesting a meeting. Some send campaign plans six months or so before publication and ask authors for feedback.

If your publisher does a lot of publicity and your book is appropriate for this treatment, consider your availability, think about how much time you are prepared to dedicate to publicity, and remember not to book your annual holiday over this crucial·period! Check your diary in advance and try to minimise prior engagements in the weeks leading up to and immediately after publication: this is when promotional activity intensifies and you may be invited on to television or radio at short notice.

Being prepared to step in at the last minute is usually worthwhile. When you are building your reputation you may not be the producer's first choice – but if a more established guest drops out this could be the opportunity you've been waiting for.

However, don't worry if you feel uneasy about guesting live on radio and television – a publicist is unlikely to try to persuade you to do anything to promote the book that you're not comfortable with. For example, radio programmes such as Woman's Hour on BBC Radio 4 may want to know in advance if an author is a confident talker who sounds good live. The publicist will know how you come across from speaking to you, and will probably only recommend you if they feel it would be beneficial for all concerned. If a live appearance wouldn't work then a pre-recorded interview could be suggested instead (provided it fits in with the overall format of the programme).

It is a good idea to watch, read and listen to the media you hope to be covered in. Daytime television shows, magazine programmes on BBC network radio, and news-paper weekend supplements are distinct in form and con-tent. Radio 4's *Start the Week* and *Midweek* are based on live panel discussions, network TV shows like *Good Morning* have a magazine format, *The Time . . . The Place* centres around topical debate. Cable and satellite channels will have equivalents.

Keep an eye on what journalists are writing about and look at how books and authors fit in to programmes and publications – explore all the possible angles.

Any information you can provide about potential media interest, or any conferences, exhibitions or regular events at which the book may be promoted is extremely valuable, and may not only help with publicity but could also be useful for direct sales initiatives. While researching and writing the book you will probably have encountered many professional people who could be useful. Advise the publicity department about them, and any relevant specialist publications, professional organisations or societies that you know of. Remember, however, to keep this realistic. Specific contacts and specialist suggestions are best – giving your publicist a list of every major national TV and radio station will not be helpful. The publicist will have in-depth professional knowledge of national mainstream media, and to a degree local and specialist outlets, while you are likely to be the expert when it comes to journalists and publications local to your area or specialising in your subject.

A lively author biography can help grab a media editor's attention, so it is worth making sure that your publicist has your personal details. If possible, it is best to give a sense of your personality rather than simply listing what you have done in a professional capacity. A good tip is to think about what captures your interest when you read about other people, and if you're happy to use it, note down any personal experience which adds to your authority on the subject. If you do have well-known friends or family members you could think about whether you'd want to use that to help generate publicity (and of course whether or not they themselves would want to be involved in this way). The publicist will let you know if they will need a publicity photo – black-and-white head-and-shoulders shots are generally the preferred format.

The publicity department starts work on books several months prior to publication. Many periodicals work up to five months in advance; similarly television programme development requires early notification. At some houses advance information sheets are sent out to major glossy magazines six months in advance of publication and this is followed by a targeted ring-round to ascertain the magazines' interest in seeing review copies. Radio, TV and newspapers are contacted later – around eight weeks prior to publication. They are sent a press release which alerts them to the book and gives them the chance to request review copies and enquire about author availability for interview. Again, the publicist may chase by phone to assess interest before review copies are sent out to key outlets and publications. If you go on an author tour then regional media will probably want to pick up on the book as it will have a local angle for them if you are appearing in their area.

How much is spent on publicity depends on the individual title. Although launches can be valuable they can be expensive and media contacts get so many invitations to such events that attendance is never guaranteed. Publishers need to ensure that money is not spent on drinks for family and friends, with little publicity or sales benefit. The publicity budget may be better spent elsewhere.

Unknown authors will have the odds stacked against them to a degree as established names obviously get more attention. With an unknown, the subject will be key, as will such aspects as topicality, uniqueness and wide general appeal. It is wise to be realistic about coverage, bearing in mind the sheer number of books being pitched to the media, and considering the attention that big names can command. If lots of reviews and interviews are not appearing, it is not necessarily the case that your publicist is not doing anything. Publishers inform authors of the work they are doing to varying degrees and not knowing what is happening does not mean that nothing is. Call your publicist – or if you don't know your publicist, your editor – and ask to be kept informed. Helpful suggestions ought always to be valued but it is wise to remember that the publicist has much experience with the media – and that she or he is likely to have drawn your book to the attention of the relevant people.

Some bigger publishers will put large publicity or promotion budgets behind a proportion of their titles. If you are lucky, this will happen to you! But most authors do not receive this treatment. Small publishers may have fewer titles and may be more able to concentrate on detailed publicity campaigns; larger houses may have more resources or money to spend. But all publishers are different. How well-resourced and/or how organised, efficient and dynamic they are may be impossible to judge before you experience them. Good luck!

Sales
Mary Hemming

Getting books into bookshops, and to the customer, is undoubtedly one of the most important stages in the publishing process: this is the time when everybody hopes to see their efforts and investment come to fruition. Books need to be made readily available to the reading public, whether it is through bookshops, libraries or other, sometimes more direct, sources. The sales department is there to ensure that happens.

The first pieces of information sent out by most sales departments are Advance Information sheets (AIs), which go to all key sales contacts. These are: the reps who will eventually be presenting the books to the shops, both in the UK and overseas; other sales agencies who will be working on the publisher's behalf; key trade customers such as major bookshops, wholesalers and library suppliers; as well as database services such as British Books in Print and Book Data. Book information is also held on CD-Rom which can include cover visuals. AIs usually cover information on a whole season of books. Where I work, AIs go out twice a year, six months in advance of the first month's titles. They contain essential details such as the title, subtitle, author, ISBN (an individual book identification number), publication date and a provisional price and, in addition to these basic details, a brief description of the book, its contents and its author, a note of expected publicity, and the main selling points.

The information which authors provide to their publisher in the early stages, such as the Author Questionnaire, will be used to compile AIs. It is worth bearing this in mind and ensuring that such information is comprehensive and includes any ideas or specific leads you may have to help promote the sales of your book.

What sells books to bookshops and the trade is often not so much what the book is about, but factors that will make it successful in the marketplace. For example, if a nationwide author tour, and extensive publicity and marketing campaigns are in the pipeline this can be announced in the AIs, along with any planned point-of-sale support in the shops, such as showcards, window displays or dump-bins (the book-trade word for the type of display case most usually used in bookshops). Of course, the kind of marketing spend will depend on each individual title: a big budget may be appropriate for a high-profile, controversial biography; for a highly specialist academic work the most likely emphasis will be on maximising sales through the relevant specialist outlets.

Publishers produce catalogues on a regular basis, usually one for each season, and these are also important sales tools. They are normally available approximately two months prior to the start of the season, so catalogues for books published from February onwards will be available from around November, for example. Like AIs, catalogues are sent to bookshops, libraries, wholesalers and educational suppliers; they are also sent in bulk to stockholding agents and distributors overseas. The catalogue will include details on the book, its author and contents, and which rights the publisher holds for each title (for an explanation of 'rights' see Dorothy Lumley and Lynette Owen's chapters). A cover visual and/or author photograph may be included along with the main text. The catalogue also often goes out to the publisher's direct mailing list, to agents and others, and is taken by the publisher to events. It is a publicity as well as a sales tool, and the material in it has less of a 'hard sell' approach than that of the AIs.

Another important fixture in the sales calendar is the publication of what is still informally called the Export *Bookseller* – the 'Autumn Books' and 'Spring Books' editions of the *Bookseller* magazine. Most publishers advertise their titles here (although with more sophisticated databases coming into use, it remains to be seen whether this will continue) and these directories are distributed to booksellers all over the world.

Despite the fact that booksellers receive AIs and catalogues from publishers and wholesalers well in advance of publication, however, many of them won't actually order copies of a book until they see the rep.

Reps are employed by publishers on different terms: some may be full-time salaried staff, working exclusively for one publisher (which is more often the case with the large multi-nationals); others will be freelance and work for several different houses on a commission basis. The information the publisher provides is crucial, at least partly because first of all it 'sells' the book to the rep.

The ideal opportunity for the enthusiastic publisher to inspire their usually notoriously cynical sales reps is at the annual (or in some cases seasonal) sales conference which will be attended by editors, in-house sales and marketing personnel and area/regional reps. At the conference commissioning editors build on the information given in the AIs and present their lists to the sales teams. This gives each department the chance to talk about the structure of the season and look at how the books interrelate, and also provides a forum where sales, marketing and promotional plans and targets can be presented and discussed.

Another major advantage of the conference is that it enables the publisher to give the reps a feel for each individual title: this is the time when any anecdotes or verbal selling points can be highlighted and cover visuals can be presented to give an idea of how the book will look.

The cover is a crucial selling tool: it alerts the buyer to the overall tone of the book, and many reps won't begin to try to present a book to a customer until they have a visual to work with. Thus, cover visuals or proofs will be provided to reps around five months in advance, or at the earliest opportunity, along with AIs and a note of anticipated publicity for each title. Reps will usually put the information and visuals for each title into a presentation folder, and when they visit a bookshop work through it with the buyer, giving the verbal presentation as they show each cover. Reps are often cynical for good reasons – they are lucky to get more than a couple of minutes to present each book to the buyer and they have to fight to keep hold of their presentation folder for fear that the buyer will wrest it out of their hands and flip through it at an alarming pace without giving the poor rep chance to draw breath. Typical comments a rep is likely to hear every day are: 'We don't have any call for that kind of book round here'; 'What a crap cover'; 'Who's Jeffrey Archer?'

The initial order the bookshop makes is called a subscription. If the rep's visit is successful the bookshop buyer or manager will decide to 'sub-in' a specified number of copies of a book usually, and certainly in general trade publishing, on a sale or return basis. The current trend in trade publishing is that the quantities of books being 'subbed-in' to bookshops is falling. In addition, shops are giving books less time before they decide to return them to a publisher as unsold stock, which means that reps are having to work harder to persuade bookshops to order sufficient quantities for display. The sale or return aspect also means that an accurate picture of the sales figures for each title will emerge only after an extended period when sales have had a chance to settle down: a proportion of sales recorded on the author's first royalty statement may later appear as a deficit if copies have been returned to the publisher.

In addition to the reps on the road, a senior sales person from the publisher will usually visit the head offices of the major accounts and wholesalers to present titles. These crucial appointments have to be set up at least six months in advance of publication and the head-office buyers will probably expect to be shown finished covers and examples of any point-of-sale or other marketing material. (This is one reason why covers have to be produced so far in advance and this has a knock-on effect for your manuscript delivery date. The publisher needs a confirmed spine width for a finished cover so your manuscript may have to be typeset many months in advance of publication.)

Your publisher will also have a network of distributors and agents overseas, all working to sell your books. For example, the company I work for has distribution arrangements in Australia, New Zealand, South Africa, America and Canada, and we have sales agents and reps throughout Europe, the Far and Middle East.

The general climate of the book trade is very unpredictable at the time of writing. Major changes are taking place and selling books is increasingly tough. Thus, any information you can provide to help sell the book could be very valuable. It's not all doom and gloom but publishers now need to be more imaginative than ever in their approach to selling. Reps work on a regional basis, so it is a good idea to ensure that your publisher knows where you live, and work, and to alert them to any local bookshops, libraries, schools, colleges or institutions which may have an interest in you and your book. If you are an academic, advise the publisher of any universities or courses which you think might be interested in adopting your book as a set text and of any conferences on your subject. Even if your book is quite general there may be organisations or institutions that you know of who could be interested in buying multiple copies to sell to their members. Any media contacts you have overseas may also be very useful. The sooner your publisher is aware of all these, the better.

Publishers may also decide to target specialist markets by mailing leaflets and order forms direct: let them know of any interested groups or organisations that you are aware of so they can be added to a direct mail-shot.

If you are taking part in any local events or conferences let your publicist know: she or he can pass on the relevant information to the sales department. Similarly, the publicity department should keep the sales department up to date on any forthcoming press coverage: whether it is in the major national media or part of a targeted local campaign. If reps can tell the bookseller that the author is appearing on national radio next Wednesday morning, promises of forthcoming appearances and publicity seem far more concrete and subscriptions or reorders are likely to increase.

If at first you don't see your book when you visit a bookshop don't be disheartened. It doesn't necessarily mean the book isn't there – with non-fiction it could be that the book is shelved in a completely different section to where you'd expect to find it. Every book does have a category printed on the back cover, but it may not fit in with the bookshop's own shelving system, or an individual buyer's conception of the title.

If, however, you have searched the shop thoroughly, and perhaps have discovered that your book isn't there, don't panic. There could be a number of reasons and the situation can often by remedied. Shops like W H Smith are very important because they are major high-street retailers and put in large orders. But they will only take books which are suitable for their shops, and those are books which appeal to a very wide general-interest market such as cookery, crafts, popular biographies and general leisure titles: highly specialist and academic texts won't be appropriate for them – local, specialist and university bookshops are far more likely to stock these. Moreover, the larger chains like W H Smith can often only order those books that their head office has rated as likely to be top sellers. If your book has not been chosen, the publisher's sales effort will have to have been concentrated elsewhere.

It is also important to be aware that just because a bookshop is local to you it doesn't necessarily mean they will be supportive, although hopefully they will be, particularly if they know you already. If they don't, you could drop in to a local bookshop to introduce yourself and the book if you wanted to – but it is always wise to make a note of the name of the person you spoke to. A bookshop manager may well reassure an author that of course they will order in plentiful copies of the book when they meet face-to-face, but when the publisher or the rep tries to follow up on the lead nobody in the shop knows a thing about it. If the person calling has the name of the person you spoke to it may help to jog their memory!

If you don't see your book in a suitable outlet, do tell your publisher. Most will be only too happy to fill a missed opportunity and get the rep on to it. It's never worth holding back from letting the publisher know about any sales opportunities you can think of; they can pay attention

or not as they see fit and in many cases you may well find
that no sale is too small!

Notes on contributors

Jane Aaron, a senior lecturer in English at the University of Wales, Aberystwyth, is the author of *A Double Singleness: Gender and the Writings of Charles and Mary Lamb*, and co-editor of *Out of the Margins: Women's Studies in the Nineties* and *Our Sisters' Land: The Changing Identities of Women in Wales*. She is currently working on a Welsh-language book on nineteenth-century Welsh women's writings.

Rebecca Abrams is an award-winning journalist and author. Her articles and reviews have appeared in many of the national newspapers and magazines, and she is a regular contributor to the *Guardian*. In 1993 she was awarded an Amnesty International Press Award. She is the author of *When Parents Die: Learning to Live with the Loss of a Parent* (Thorsons, 1992), shortlisted for the 1996 MIND book of the year award; *Woman in a Man's World: Pioneering Career Women of the Twentieth Century* (Methuen, 1993); and *Play Rights: The Issue Feminism Forgot* (forthcoming). She is currently researching women's friendships.

Frances Arnold has worked in non-fiction publishing for the past 12 years and is currently a senior editor at Macmillan with responsibility for commissioning social science textbooks for students and professionals. She has also written a non-fiction book for children, *Greece: World in View* (Heinemann, 1991), and has edited several travel guides.

Judith Baxter is a lecturer of English in Education at the University of Reading with a particular interest in language and gender. She has written a number of course-books for schools including *English for GCSE: A Course for Further Education* (Cambridge University Press, 1989) and *Making Meaning: GCSE English for Schools* (Cambridge University Press, 1990). She is the editor of the *Wildfire* series of women's writing for schools, and she is presently editing *Cambridge Literature For Schools*, a series of texts for GCSE and A level.

Alex Bennion graduated in Medieval and Modern History from Liverpool University before entering publishing as an editor. She specialised for many years in works of non-fiction, in subjects ranging from politics, history and biography to psychology, self-help and environmental issues. In addition, she has written book reviews and articles, and compiled two anthologies: *The Comedy Collection* and *The Essential Book of Poetry*. She is now a senior editor with a major London trade publisher.

Christine Pedotti Bonnel has worked as a freelance journalist and writer and is the editor of several book lists. Her encyclopedia of Catholicism for children and young adults was published in 1994.

Gill Davies is currently managing director of Free Association Books Ltd, a small independent publisher specialising in academic and professional books in the social and behavioural sciences. She was previously managing director of Tavistock Publications and Library Association

Publishing, and Publishing Director for Routledge. She was the first woman to be elected Chair of the Council of Academic and Professional Publishing with the Publishers Association, and is honorary lecturer in Publishing at Cardiff University. Her book, *Book Commissioning and Acquisition* (Blueprint, 1994) discusses in detail what an editor's work entails, and how editors work as part of teams within publishing houses.

Hanna Diamond is Jean Monnet Lecturer in French History at the University of Bath. Her research has focused on women's experiences of World War Two in the Toulouse area of France. She is the author of several articles on the subject and continues to be interested in using interviews for research, particularly in the context of oral history. Her current work concerns the lives of French immigrant women.

Mary Hemming worked as a social worker and community worker in Glasgow and ran the Glasgow Women's Centre bookstall, before taking her first job in the book trade in the mid-1970s. She became half of the Scottish branch of Publications Distribution Co-operative, the first broad-based British radical book distributor, and repped the very first titles from The Women's Press, among many other lists. She was a founder member of Scottish and Northern Book Distribution Co-operative, and of Stramullion, the Scottish feminist publishers. In 1983 she joined The Women's Press, where she is now Sales and Joint Managing Director. She has been active in lesbian feminist politics for twenty years and co-edited, with Jan Bradshaw, *Girls Next Door: Lesbian Feminist Stories* (The Women's Press, 1985).

Dorothy Lumley's first job was as editorial assistant in a reference magazine in the days of cowgum and galley proofs. New English Library took her on as paperback editor, and at Magnum/Methuen paperbacks she was editorial director. She has had two stints as freelance reader/copy-editor. Life as an agent began at Laurence Pollinger Ltd then, after moving to Devon, she launched her own Dorian Literary Agency in 1986. She is also a published writer of romantic fiction.

Virginia Masardo was born in India and trained as a journalist and editor. She has worked as a freelance copy-editor and proofreader for the past ten years, specialising in educational, professional and reference texts. She is a founder member of the Society of Freelance Editors and Proofreaders and is currently reading for a part-time degree in Modern European Studies at University College, London.

Karen McCarthy has worked in publishing and the media for over ten years, as an editor, broadcaster and publicist. She has worked as a news reporter in local radio and as a freelance journalist for BBC World Service and BBC Radio 4, and is currently a Publicity Manager at Cassell plc. She is a graduate of Middlesex University and also a published poet.

Wendy Mercer has taught at universities in France and England and is currently at University College, London. Her publications include editions of *Voyage d'une femme au Spitzburg* and *Jane Osborn*, both by Léonie d'Aunet. She is currently preparing a biography of Xavier Marmier, as well as translating and editing a collection of short stories by nineteenth-century French women writers.

Lynette Owen is rights and contracts director of Addison

Wesley Longman, an educational and academic publishing group. She is the author of *Selling Rights* (Blueprint, Chapman and Hall, 2nd/edn., 1994) and lectures regularly in the United Kingdom and abroad on copyright and licensing matters.

Sue Roe worked as a freelance writer and editor for two academic publishers before taking up her current post as lecturer in Creative Writing at the University of East Anglia. Her non-fiction publications include *Writing and Gender: Virginia Woolf's Writing Practice* (Harvester Wheatsheaf, 1990); the Penguin Modern Classics edition of Virginia Woolf's *Jacob's Room* (1992); and *The Semi-Transparent Envelope: Women Writing – Feminism and Fiction* (with Susan Sellers and Nicole Ward Jouve, Marian Boyars, 1994).

Gerrilyn Smith is a clinical psychologist and systemic therapist, offering training, consultancy and clinical services. She works predominantly with women and children and specialises in the treatment of the survivors of physical and sexual violence. She is the author of three books, including *Dealing With Depression*, with Kathy Nairne, and *The Protector's Handbook: Preventing Child Sexual Abuse and Helping Children Recover*, both published by The Women's Press.

Moira Taylor is the Textbook Development Editor at Routledge. She has worked as a journalist, reviewer, editor and music administrator. She produced and narrated a radio documentary on contemporaries of Katherine Mansfield, and organised the 'New Zealand Women in Literature 1890–1975' exhibition for the United Women's Convention at the University of Canterbury, Christchurch.

Heather Young Leslie is a Canadian anthropologist who has travelled and researched in North and Central America, Europe and the South Pacific. Her current interests include cross-cultural understandings of health, gender and motherhood. She is a lecturer on the Midwifery Education Programme at McMaster University in Hamilton, Ontario, where she lives.

Select bibliography

Banks, Michael and Dibell, Ansen, *Word Processing Secrets for Writers*, Writer's Digest Books, Cincinnati, Ohio, 1989

Barrass, Robert, *Scientists Must Write: A Guide to Better Writing for Scientists and Engineers*, Chapman and Hall, London, 1978

Blackwell Guide for Authors, Blackwell, Oxford, 1985

Blain, Virginia, Clements, Patricia and Grundy, Isobel (eds), *The Feminist Companion to Literature in English*, Batsford, London, 1990

Bolt, David, *An Author's Handbook*, Piatkus Books, London, 1986

Briggs, Jean, *Never in Anger: Portrait of an Eskimo Family*, Harvard University Press, Cambridge, Ma., 1970

Burgess, Robert, *In the Field: An Introduction to Field Research*, Allen and Unwin, London, 1984

Butcher, Judith, *The Cambridge Handbook: Copy-editing for Editors, Authors, Publishers*, 3rd edn. revd., Cambridge University Press, Cambridge, 1992

The Cassell Directory of Publishing, Cassell, in association with the Publishers' Association (published annually)

Campbell, Morag, *Writing About Travel*, A. and C. Black, London, 1995

Chamberlain, Mary (ed), *Writing Lives: Conversations Between Women Writers*, Virago, London, 1988

Chicago Manual of Style, 13th edn., University of Chicago Press, Chicago, 1982

Clark, Charles (ed), *Publishing Agreements: A Book of Precedents*, 4th edn., Butterworths, London, 1993

Clark, Giles, *Inside Book Publishing*, Blueprint, London, 1994

Clayton, Joan, *Interviewing For Journalists*, Piatkus, London, 1994

Curran, Susan, *How to Write a Book and Get it Published*, Thorsons, London, 1990

Danziger, N., *Danziger's Travels: Beyond Forbidden Frontiers*, Grafton, London, 1987

Davies, Gill, *Book Commissioning and Acquisition*, Blueprint, London, 1994

Delton, Judy, *The 29 Most Common Writing Mistakes (And How to Avoid Them,)* Writer's Digest Books, Cincinatti, Ohio, 1990

Dorner, Jane, 'Authors and Information Technology', *New Challenges in Publishing*, Dorner BNB Research Fund Report 52, British Library, 1991

——*Writing on Disk: An A–Z Handbook of Terms, Tips and Techniques for Authors and Publishers*, John Taylor Book Ventures AQ place, 1992

Doyle, Margaret, *The A–Z of Non-Sexist Language*, The Women's Press, London, 1995

Emerson, Robert, *Contemporary Field Research: A Collection of Readings*, Little, Brown and Company, Toronto, 1983

Fowler, H. W., *A Dictionary of Modern English Usage*, 2nd edn., revised by Sir Ernest Gowers, Oxford University Press, Oxford, 1965

Gluck, Sherna Berger and Patai, Daphne (eds), *Women's Words: The Feminist Practice of Oral History*, Routledge, London, 1991

Harts' Rules for Compositors and Readers, 38th edn. revd., Oxford University Press, Oxford, 1978

Heilbrun, Carolyn G., *Writing a Woman's Life*, The Women's Press, London, 1989

Henige, David, *Oral Historiography*, Longman, London, 1982

Hines, John, *The Way to Write Non-Fiction*, Elm Tree Books, London, 1990

Hoffmann, Ann, *Research for Writers*, A. and C. Black, London, 1992

Ingham, Christine, *Working Well at Home*, Thorsons, London, 1995

Kramarae, Cheris and Treichler, Paula, *A Feminist Dictionary*, Pandora, London, 1985

Lane, Maggie, *Literary Daughters*, Hale, London, 1989

Legat, Michael, *The Nuts and Bolts of Writing*, Hale, London, 1989

——*An Author's Guide to Publishing*, Hale, London, 1992

——*Understanding Publishers' Contracts*, Hale, London, 1992

——*Non-Fiction Books: A Writer's Guide*, Hale, London, 1993

——*The Writer's Rights*, A. and C. Black, London, 1995

Manda, Ceasara, *Reflections of a Woman Anthropologist: No Hiding Place*, Academic Press, London, 1982

McCallum, Chris, *How to Write for Publication*, 3rd edn., How To Books, Plymouth, 1995

Miller, Casey and Swift, Kate, *The Handbook of Non-Sexist Writing for Writers, Editors and Speakers*, 3rd edn., The Women's Press, London, 1995

Mulvany, Nancy, *Indexing Books*, University of Chicago Press, Chicago, 1994

Olsen, Tillie, *Silences*, Virago, London, 1980

Owen, Lynette, *Selling Rights*, 2nd edn., Blueprint, Chapman and Hall, London, 1994

The Oxford Dictionary for Writers and Editors, Clarendon Press, Oxford, 1981

Perrot, Michelle (ed), *Writing Women's History*, Blackwell, Oxford, 1992

Rabinow, Paul, *Reflections on Field Work in Morocco*, University of California Press, Berkeley, 1977

Roberts, Helen (ed), *Doing Feminist Research*, Routledge, London, 1981

Ross, Tom and Marilyn, *The Complete Guide to Self-Publishing*, Writer's Digest Books, Cincinatti, Ohio, 1994

Russ, Joanna, *How to Suppress Women's Writing*, The Women's Press, London, 1984

Schumacher, Michael, *The Complete Writer's Guide to Conducting Interviews*, Writer's Digest Books, Cincinnati, Ohio, 1990

Sellers, Susan (ed), *Delighting the Heart: A Notebook by Women Writers*, The Women's Press, London, 1989

——*Taking Reality by Surprise: Writing for Pleasure and Publication*, The Women's Press, London, 1991

——*The Semi-Transparent Envelope: Women Writing – Feminism and Fiction* (with Sue Roe and Nicole Ward Jouve), Marion Boyars, London, 1994

Shattock, Joanne (ed), *The Oxford Guide to British Women Writers*, Oxford University Press, Oxford, 1993

Smedley, Christine, Allen, Mitchell and associates, *Getting Your Book Published*, Sage, London, 1993

Spender, Dale, *The Writing or the Sex? Or Why You Don't Have to Read Women's Writing to Know it's No Good*, Pergamon, New York, 1989

Spicer, Robert, *How to Publish a Book*, How To Books, Plymouth, 1993

Thompson, Paul, *The Voice of the Past: Oral History*, Oxford University Press, Oxford, 1988

Todd, Janet (ed), *A Dictionary of British and American Women Writers 1660–1800*, Methuen, London, 1987

Turner, Barry (ed), *The Writer's Handbook*, Macmillan, London, 1995

Warhol, Robyn and Herndl, Diane Price (eds), *Feminisms: An Anthology of Literary Theory and Criticism*, Rutgers University Press, New Jersey, 1991

Wells, Gordon, *The Successful Author's Handbook*, Macmillan, London, 1989

Wright, Sally-Jane, *How to Write and Sell Interviews*, Alison and Busby, London, 1995

Writers' and Artists' Yearbook, A. and C. Black, London, 1995

The Women's Press is Britain's leading women's publishing house. Established in 1978, we publish high-quality fiction and non-fiction from outstanding women writers worldwide. Our exciting and diverse list includes literary fiction, detective novels, biography and autobiography, health, women's studies, handbooks, literary criticism, psychology and self help, the arts, our popular Livewire Books series for young women and the bestselling annual *Women Artists Diary* featuring beautiful colour and black-and-white illustrations from the best in contemporary women's art.

If you would like more information about our books or about our mail order book club, please send an A5 sae for our latest catalogue and complete list to:

The Sales Department
The Women's Press Ltd
34 Great Sutton Street
London EC1V 0DX
Tel: 0171 251 3007
Fax: 0171 608 1938

Also of interest:

Susan Sellers, editor
Delighting the Heart
A Notebook by Women Writers

With Alice Walker, Emma Tennant, Hélène Cixous, Nicole Ward Jouve, and many more...

Seventeen of the world's most famous women writers discuss with candour how they approach a new piece of work, how they begin to write, and how they then develop their project. From first idea to publication of a finished piece, they offer rare and detailed insights into the process of writing across a range of genres.

'Well worth forking out for... *Delighting the Heart* is one of those rare glimpses into the way writers write. More than a glimpse: it is a thorough probing of every stage.' *Literary Review*

Creative Writing/Literary Theory £8.99
ISBN 0 7043 4167 0

Susan Sellers, editor
Taking Reality by Surprise
Writing for Pleasure and Publication

With Michèle Roberts, Zoë Fairbairns, Joan Riley, Caeia March, Amryl Johnson, and many, many more...

Over fifty editors, literary agents and writing tutors, as well as novelists, journalists, poets and playwrights – all leaders in their field – offer a complete guide to writing and getting published for accomplished and aspiring writers alike.

From starting out to choosing the appropriate genre, from finding the right outlet to keeping the momentum going, here is a wealth of advice, hands-on exercises and useful contacts.

'Gets enthusiasts past the "I've always wanted to write but..." stage. Excellent.' *Daily Telegraph*

Creative Writing £8.99
ISBN 0 7043 4267 7

Joanna Russ
How to Suppress Women's Writing

Explosive, irreverent, angry and very funny, *How to Suppress Women's Writing* exposes the backlash against women who dare to write.

Joanna Russ reveals how women's literary tradition has been systematically belittled in the past and how the prejudices that drove George Eliot and the Brontës to disguise themselves behind male pseudonyms are still alive and well today. But *How to Suppress Women's Writing* is also a celebration of women's impressive literary heritage as Joanna Russ analyses how (and why) women's writing is now breaking exciting new ground in content and style.

'You should snatch up this book...which should be rammed down the throat of every literary critic.'
New Statesman

'*How to Suppress Women's Writing* glows with racy incandescence... Her polemic has all the cunning merciless clarity of fine art.'
Washington Post

'A book of the most profound and original clarity... The study of literature should never be the same again.'
Marge Piercy

Literary Criticism/Women's Studies £6.99
ISBN 0 7043 3932 3

Carolyn G Heilbrun
Writing a Woman's Life

There are an increasing number of biographies and autobiographies of women; and novels which are seen to reflect the women writers' own lives. But how much do these books show the real lives of women; and how much are the authors concerned with having to show women in a conventional or acceptable light?

Why is it that generations of writers described George Sand as 'a great man'? Why did Dorothy L Sayers, having created a heroine as independent as herself, promptly marry her off? And why did Carolyn Heilbrun herself resort to the pseudonym of Amanda Cross to write her own detective fiction?

With fascinating insights into the lives of such unconventional women as Virginia Woolf, Colette, George Eliot, Adrienne Rich and many more, Carolyn Heilbrun examines how their stories have been distorted by assumptions about women; and charts the development of writing about women's lives. *Writing a Woman's Life* is a landmark in literary criticism and an exciting and enlightening read.

'A provocative study .' Booknews

'Compelling.' Kirkus Review

Literary Criticism £7.99
ISBN 0 7043 4184 0

The Women's Press Handbook Series

Margaret Doyle
The A-Z of Non-Sexist Language

Bringing today's vocabulary completely up-to-date, here is a
definitive guide to non-sexist language.

With a complete listing of sexist words and their non-sexist
alternatives; vital clarification of common-usage words – outlining
fully why some words are sexist and others are not; full cross-
referencing; and an easy-to-use A-Z dictionary format, here is an
invaluable handbook for writers, editors, teachers, speakers and
all who care about the words they use.

Reference/Language   £6.99
ISBN 0 7043 4430 0

The Women's Press Handbook Series

Casey Miller and Kate Swift
**The Handbook of Non-Sexist Writing
for Writers, Editors and Speakers**
Third British Edition – Fully revised and updated

How can we avoid sexist language and find clear and elegant
ways of saying what we mean? In this definitive handbook, Casey
Miller and Kate Swift offer essential solutions to the use of sexist
clichés, suffixes, prefixes, pronouns, titles, categories and terms.
Now fully revised and updated, here is a lively and informative
companion for any writer, journalist, teacher, editor and lover of
the English language.

'An essential aid for anyone who makes his or her living
out of words, as well as a sensible guide for people who
know that an even-handed language would help towards
an even-handed world.' *Cosmopolitan*

Reference/Language/Women's Studies £7.99
ISBN 0 7043 4442 4

Carolyn G Heilbrun
Hamlet's Mother and Other Women
Feminist Essays on Literature

Winner of the NCRW Writer of Distinction Award

Carolyn Heilbrun is among the most perceptive and articulate of contemporary feminist literary critics, renowned for her passion for women's writing and her subtle appreciation of how this affects and is affected by women's lives. In this superb volume, she examines the lives and work of Louisa M Alcott, May Sarton, Vera Brittain, Winifred Holtby, Dorothy L Sayers, Virginia Woolf and many more; provides an entertaining and fascinating analysis of women's crime fiction; and looks at the professional position of contemporary women within the field of literary criticism.

She also includes her groundbreaking essay on Hamlet's mother, in which she challenges the established view of Gertrude as the epitome of woman's frailty, and analyses her on the model of a Shakespearean tragic hero instead – the fine character flawed by a single weakness. This essay forever changed feminist literary criticism.

Literary criticism £7.95
ISBN 0 7043 4273 1

May Sarton
Writings on Writing

'In the end what is most difficult becomes most easy, what was heaviest to lift becomes light as air...and this happens, of course, when we are not thinking of ourselves at all, but have become instruments of our craft...'

From the first, May Sarton has been passionately committed to the art of writing. Poet, novelist, essayist and diarist, she has explored to the full the boundaries and possibilities of each literary medium. Now May Sarton turns her attention to the subject of writing itself, reflecting on the craft to which she has devoted a lifetime of endeavour. This unique and lucid volume brings together May Sarton's writings on writing in an invaluable gift to authors and readers, as, with rare insight and honesty, she shares her knowledge of her craft and art.

'Sarton has always been, in the most fruitful sense, a transgressor of boundaries: of geography, of culture, of time, of gender, and of genre... Sarton has made her distinctive literary mark.' *Sunday Times*

'One of those writers who is loved, almost as a personal friend, by readers who fall under her spell.' *Guardian*

Literature £5.99
ISBN 0 7043 4456 4

Virginia Woolf
On Women and Writing
Her Essays, Assessments and Arguments
Selected and introduced by Michèle Barrett

Virginia Woolf is famous for her novels and as the *doyenne* of the
Bloomsbury Set. Less well-known is that she was also widely
respected in her time as a major essayist and critic, with a particular interest in and commitment to women's literature. Now,
for the first time, this groundbreaking volume brings together
Virginia Woolf's essays and other critical writings.

This superb book includes Woolf's unique appraisals of the work
of such major literary figures as Jane Austen, George Eliot, the
Brontës, Mrs Gaskell, Olive Schreiner, Aphra Behn, Mary
Wollstonecraft, the Duchess Newcastle, Dorothy Richardson and
Katherine Mansfield; previously unpublished journal extracts and
commentaries on 'Women and Fiction', 'Professions for Women',
'The Intellectual Status of Women'; and much, much more.

Literature £7.99
ISBN 0 7043 3839 4

Alice Walker
The Same River Twice
Honoring the Difficult

Her first-ever full-length work of autobiography

Alice Walker was a peaceful, reclusive poet and writer when her
life was interrupted by the appearance of three extraordinary
gifts: a widely praised and bestselling novel (*The Color Purple*), the
Pulitzer Prize, and an offer from Steven Spielberg to make her
novel into a film that would become a major international event.
The Same River Twice: Honoring the Difficult chronicles the period
of transition from recluse to public figure, and invites us to con-
template, along with Alice Walker, the true significance of extraordinary gifts – especially when they are coupled, as in Walker's
case, with the most severe criticism, overt hostility, and public
censure. Looking back at her life at that time, Alice Walker asks
how the private and public mesh during periods of intense cre-
ativity and stress; the ways in which they support or weaken
each other.

Including entries from Alice Walker's personal journals and letters; essays and articles that document the controversy in the
Black community; and Alice Walker's previously unpublished
original screenplay for *The Color Purple*, *The Same River Twice:
Honoring the Difficult* offers a rich opportunity to understand how
an artist may operate in and engage the popular culture, and a
candid look at some of the pleasures and the costs.

Autobiography/Memoir £16.99
ISBN 0 7043 5070 X